MW00679440

Professional Tips and Techniques Series

Lube, Oil & Chassis Service

A mini-course for the do-it-yourselfer who wants to learn how to do it right.

Do-It-Right Publishing, Inc.
Van Nuys, California

Published and distributed by

Do-It-Right Publishing, Inc.
Post Office Box 839
Newhall, CA 91322-0839

Written by:	Michael Bishop
	Dennis Holmes
Series Concept & Design by:	Dennis Holmes
Production by:	Steve Janowski
Photography by:	Michael Bishop
	Patrick Holmes
Illustration by:	Steve Amos

FIRST EDITION
First printing, 1991
Second printing,1992

Library of Congress Card Number: 91-71747

ISBN 1-879110-16-4

Proudly printed in the United States of America.

10 9 8 7 6 5 4 3

FOREWORD

This book covers some of the most important jobs that DIYer's do: engine oil and filter changes, transmission service, lubrication, cooling system flushing, belt replacement, hose replacement, and the easier jobs on the brake, suspension, and exhaust systems.

These are the jobs that keep an engine and chassis running in top shape for a long reliable life. And by doing the work yourself, you will save a lot of money on parts, lubricants, and labor. Usually, you will "earn" $15-25 per hour for the type of work taught in this book!

A major goal of the book is to give you a broad understanding of lubrication and chassis service work. From over 18 years of producing official factory shop manuals and technician training programs, we've distilled what we feel is the most important "wisdom" of the experts, and put it into this one small book.

We tell you which jobs have a good payoff for the DIYer and which jobs you should steer clear of. We show you the most common mistakes and how to avoid them.

We've tried to give you the experience of looking over the shoulder of a pro as he works, to learn more about *what* he does and *why*. The hundreds of photos and illustrations in the book *show* you the techniques, short-cuts, and quality tips that are used by factory-trained professional technicians.

Be sure to study the *Pro Tips* that are scattered throughout the book. These are tidy treatments of topics that never seem to fit into a regular shop manual, but that are important elements in the overall knowledge of a professional technician.

This is a *job-specific* book, rather than a vehicle-specific book. This means that it focuses on teaching you specific job skills rather than just procedures. In reading this book, let your mind be tuned-in to getting the *big picture.* You will learn how things work and how to get quality results. What you learn will help you not just with the one vehicle that you're working on today, but with *all* the vehicles in the family and all the vehicles you'll be working on in the future!

In short, this is a mini-course on lubrication and chassis service for the DIYer! We hope it builds your skill, improves the quality and speed of your work, and saves you some big money.

THANKS

Thanks to our partners—Steve McKee, Lonetta Holmes, and John Dawson. They gave us the enthusiastic encouragement we needed to launch this new series of books.

Thanks to Vance Lausmann for his technical review and for contributing the section on oil additives and synthetic oils. Thanks to Robert Beck for his technical review and helpful comments.

Thanks to Bert Poncher for freely sharing his 25 years of experience in the automotive aftermarket and helping shape the direction of this Professional Tips and Techniques series.

Thanks to Jana Brett for her assistance in cover design. Thanks to Dan Hackett and Karl Anthony for their technical assistance with Ventura Publisher.

Thanks to Nissan Motor Corporation in U.S.A. and Hyundai Motor America for their support and endorsement of our model-specific series of manuals. They have helped validate our highly visual approach to this type of book, and they have made a lot of their customers quite happy in the process.

And thanks to the 35,000+ professional technicians in Toyota, Nissan, Honda, and Hyundai dealerships for whom we have developed factory training programs and manuals over the past 18 years. It was *you* who taught, and we who learned.

THE SPECIFICATIONS YOU NEED

The most important specifications you will need to do the jobs in this book are fluid capacities and type. In other words, how many quarts of oil for your engine, how many quarts of automatic transmission fluid, gallons of coolant, and so forth. The best place to find these capacities is in your Owner's Manual.

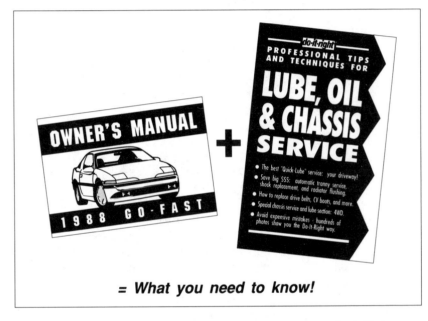

= What you need to know!

Your Owner's Manual plus this Do-It-Right book equals what you need to know for normal lube, oil-change, and chassis service.

If for any reason you don't have the Owner's Manual for one of your vehicles, see page 6 for how to obtain another copy. They are usually quite inexpensive.

Contents At-a-Glance

Detailed Contents

IMPORTANT SAFETY NOTICE

Pay special heed to the *warnings* in this book. They are intended to help protect you and your vehicle. When lifting your vehicle, make sure it is securely supported on jackstands before performing any work underneath it. Do *not* rely on the jack that came with your car or truck for safe support.

You should use standard and accepted safety precautions and equipment when handling toxic or flammable fluids. You should wear safety goggles or other protection during cutting, grinding, chiseling, prying, or any other similar process that can cause material removal or projectiles.

Following proper service procedures is essential for your safety and the correct functioning of your vehicle. We believe that the general service procedures in this book are described in such a manner that they may be performed safely and properly on a wide variety of vehicles. However, it is your responsibility to determine the precise applicability of these procedures to your specific vehicle or engine.

Please note that the condition of your vehicle, or the level of your mechanical skill, or your level of reading comprehension may result in or contribute in some way to an occurrence which causes injury to yourself or damage to your vehicle. It is not possible to anticipate all of the conceivable ways or conditions under which cars and trucks may be serviced, or to provide warnings as to all of the possible hazards that may result. Accordingly, because of these conditions which are unknown to us and are beyond our control, our liability must be and is limited to the cost of this book.

If you use service procedures, tools, or parts which are not specifically recommended in this book you must first completely satisfy yourself that neither your safety nor the safety of your vehicle will be jeopardized. All liability is expressly disclaimed for any injury or damage if you fail in any respect to follow all of the instructions and warnings given in any procedure in this book.

Although the information in this book is based on industry sources and experts, it is possible that changes in designs may be made which could not be included here. While striving for precise accuracy, Do-It-Right Publishing, Inc. cannot assume responsibility for any errors, changes, or omissions that may occur in the information presented here.

Section 1:

Save Money With Frequent Maintenance

DOES YOUR VEHICLE NEED MORE FREQUENT MAINTENANCE THAN THE FACTORY RECOMMENDS?

We recommend more frequent maintenance than auto manufacturers do. We're concerned with more than just the first 50,000 miles; we want to help you enjoy trouble free operation well past 100,000 miles! We think you should have the option of keeping your car or truck for many years without worrying about the cost of a major rebuild or new-car payments. And, when you do trade in or sell, we want you to get top dollar for your well-maintained cream puff.

The official factory maintenance schedule for your car or truck is included in your Owner's Manual. Schedules vary for a number of reasons: year-to-year changes in state and federal standards; individual vehicle needs; midyear changes; California versus 49-state models. For these reasons, it's essential that you understand the schedule for your vehicle.

Manufacturers are under a lot of pressure to produce the lowest *Cost of Ownership* in the first 50,000 miles, because this is information that is published by the government for consumer comparison purposes. So, they recommend the *least maintenance* possible for the lowest cost-of-ownership number. Typically, you will find recommendations of 6,000- to 7,500- mile intervals between oil, filter, lube, and inspection jobs for *normal* driving. We think this is way too long.

IS YOUR VEHICLE SUBJECTED TO SEVERE SERVICE?

The manufacturers wisely recommend much more frequent maintenance for "severe" driving conditions. What is "severe?" Read the following list of severe conditions and ask yourself if at least one item does not apply to you:

■ **Repeated short-distance driving—trips of less than 5 miles or 10 minutes.** The engine and drive train aren't warmed up completely; carbon tends to build up in the combustion chambers; acids are produced by condensation and contaminate the oil.

■ **Extreme low-temperature operation—when outside temperatures remain below freezing.** Rapid cooling of the engine and transmission lead to excessive condensation. This produces contamination in the engine oil and transmission fluid.

- **Extensive idling or sustained low-speed driving—like police, taxi, or door-to-door delivery use.** A tendency toward mixture richness at idle washes the cylinder walls and contaminates the oil with fuel and combustion by-products.

- **Driving in dusty conditions.** Dust clogs the air filter, and contaminates the oil and other lubricants.

- **Driving rough, muddy, or salt-spread roads.** The entry of water past seals and the buildup of mud and salt deposits lead to rust and corrosion damage of bearings, suspension components, and frame and body.

- **Towing a trailer, using a car top carrier.** The increased constant load causes the engine and drive train to work harder, accelerating wear and the breakdown of lubricants.

Did you find that one or more of the above items apply to your driving? Then you should follow the schedule in your vehicle Owner's Manual for "severe driving conditions." Usually, this means cutting maintenance intervals in half—from, say, 7,500 miles to 3,750 miles. We take that interval just a little further...

Lube, Oil, & Chassis Service

WHAT WE RECOMMEND

As a do-it-yourselfer, you have two things going for you that the factory didn't reckon on:

1. You can perform excellent maintenance for about 75% less cost.

2. You care about keeping your vehicle for 100,000 miles and well beyond.

For the do-it-yourselfer it makes no sense to stretch oil and filter changes. Given the high cost of new vehicles, the high cost of repairs, and the desirability of long life and reliability, don't scrimp on the cheapest, easiest jobs you can do. Over the long haul, you will save a substantial amount of money with more frequent maintenance.

We recommend that your basic service interval for oil change, lubrication, and inspection be *every 3,000 miles or every 3 months*, whichever comes first. This is simple and easy to remember. It will save you money.

IF YOUR VEHICLE IS UNDER WARRANTY: KEEP RECORDS OF YOUR MAINTENANCE

If your vehicle is under warranty, you can do your own maintenance and still keep the warranty in effect. Make sure that you perform all of the tasks that are shown in the maintenance schedule; do them on time or more frequently than recommended. Make sure you keep a written record of everything you do, and save all sales receipts for oil, fluids, filters, etc. In the event of a warranty-related problem you may be required to prove that required maintenance was performed.

To help you keep an accurate maintenance record, we've provided a maintenance log at the back of this book. The sample entries shown below correctly document work performed. Notice that in addition to such entries as date and mileage, space is also provided for notes that might have a bearing on why and how the work was performed.

Maintenance Log

Date/Mileage	Work Performed	Parts/Supplies Used*	Cost
10/3/90	OIL/FILTER CHANGE	4 QT. 10W-50	$4.66
18662	LUBE	PF 30 FILTER	$3.45
11/26/90	OIL/FILTER CHANGE	4 QT. 10W-50	$4.66
20205	LUBE	PF30 FILTER	$3.45
	CHANGE THERMOSTAT	THERMOSTAT (190°F)	$3.14
	FLUSH SYSTEM/ CHANGE COOLANT	1 CAN FLUSH	$2.85
		2 GAL. ANTIFR.	$9.12
1/12/91	TUNE-UP	8 FT44S PLUGS	$9.66
	CHECK TIMING - OK CHECK IDLE - OK	PCV Valve	$3.24

NEED AN OWNER'S MANUAL?

We recommend that you have an Owner's Manual for every vehicle in your family. It provides useful information on recommended maintenance schedules, oil specifications, coolant and fluid capacities, etc. (Most of this information is also available where you buy auto parts.)

Over 95% of the vehicles on the road have their Owner's Manuals in the glovebox. But if you are one of the unfortunate few who have lost it, call your local dealership or the manufacturer for a replacement. (Typical cost, $5 to $10.)

Most vehicle manufacturers have a toll-free 800 number that you can obtain by calling Directory Assistance: 1-800-555-1212. Ask for the Customer Assistance or Customer Service department of the manufacturer of your vehicle.

PRO TIP: Don't Miss the Warranty Coverage You May Not Know You Have

Wouldn't you know it? Your 36-month/36,000-mile warranty ran out last week and you just learned that the poor performance, rough idle, and stalling you've been experiencing the last two days is because the "brain" for the fuel injection is faulty. And your favorite garage wants $500 to replace it!

Well, cheer up. That electronic control module—the brain—is an emissions-related system. As such it's covered under a separate Federally mandated warranty for 50,000 miles (70,000 miles for some parts), so your next stop should be your dealer.

Here's a quick-reference list for emissions-related parts and systems. Check the warranty for your vehicle. There may be others:

- Carburetor and internal parts
- Electronic fuel injection
- Diesel fuel injection pump and nozzles
- Cold-start enrichment system
- Deceleration controls
- Idle speed control system
- Exhaust manifold
- Spark plugs, ignition coil, and wires (California only)
- Altitude compensation system
- Catalytic converter
- Distributor and internal parts
- Spark advance/retard system
- Vapor storage canister and liquid separator
- Fuel filler neck restrictor and check valve
- Fuel tank and filler cap

- PCV (positive crankcase ventilation) system

- Oil filler cap

- Turbocharger (California only)

- Throttle chamber (California only)

- Air flow meter (California only)

- EGR (exhaust gas recirculation) control valve and system

- Exhaust air induction system

- Hoses, clamps, fittings, and tubing used in the above systems

- Vacuum-, temperature-, and time-sensitive valves and switches used in the above systems

- Electronic controls used in the above systems

If anything goes wrong in the first 50,000 miles in any of these systems, check with your new-car dealer for emissions system warranty coverage. (Some components are covered for 70,000 miles.)

Even if you are not the original owner of your vehicle, you still have this coverage. It transfers automatically to all subsequent owners of the vehicle.

Section 2:

Parts, Supplies, and Tools

The "shopping list" shown on the following pages will help you get all of the things you need before you begin work.

When buying tools, parts, and supplies, it's smart to go with "name" brands. Products that have been around for a long time are generally very competitive. They offer good quality, suitability, and reasonable price. If they didn't, they wouldn't survive.

You may already own many of the tools you'll need to do the jobs in this book. But if you don't, we recommend that you buy only those you'll need for the jobs you plan to do.

Lube, Oil, & Chassis Service

Engine oil—Buy only quality oil with an API (American Petroleum Institute) rating of SG. We recommend a multigrade viscosity, suitable for your location and season.

Oil filter—Buy only a quality filter. Make certain it is the correct one for your engine—and your vehicle. Taller "heavy-duty" filters may not fit in some applications. Check the directory you'll find in the filter section of the store or ask a parts counterman.

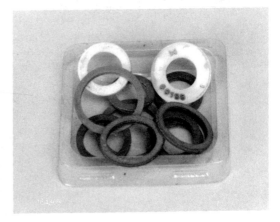

Drain plug washer—Available in auto parts stores, plastic drain plug washers should be replaced at each oil change. Copper washers are usually good for several changes.

Drain pan—*It should be larger than the capacity of your engine. Convenient drain-and-store pans make it easy to transport old oil to a recycling station.*

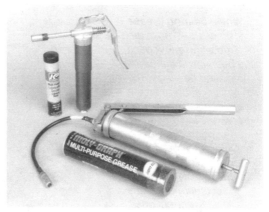

Grease gun—*A small cartridge gun, like the one on the left, is inexpensive and dependable. A larger gun is more economical if you have several vehicles to care for. A flexible end is helpful for hard-to-reach fittings.*

Grease—multipurpose—*This type is excellent for suspension lubrication. If you have a cartridge grease gun, you'll need a cartridge type refill, and if your gun is a bulk type, you will need a can of grease.*

High-temperature grease—This is for wheel bearings on vehicles equipped with disc brakes, and can be used on other wheel bearings as well.

Wheel bearing grease seals—These are required when you repack the bearings in hubs with unsealed bearings. The old seal must be pried out to remove, clean, and grease the inner bearing. See page 78, "How to service wheel bearings," to see if you need seals. If you do, ask your parts counterman for the correct ones.

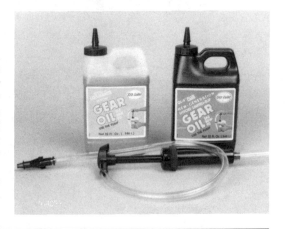

Manual transmission and differential gear oil—Your vehicle may require different weights for the transmission and for the differential. Check your Owner's Manual for the correct viscosities. Also check to see if you need lube for a limited-slip differential.

Transmission fluid—automatic—This will be either Type A (DEXRON) or Type F, depending on your transmission. Check your Owner's Manual.

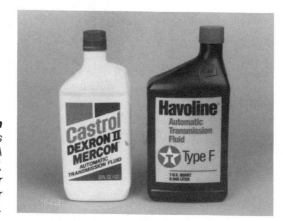

Drive belts—Check with your auto parts store for the correct types and sizes. And keep the old ones for spares.

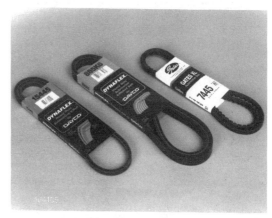

Cooling system flush—Use regular strength for routine service, or heavy-duty strength to remove heavy corrosion and scale.

Antifreeze—Buy it when it's on sale and save. You need half the amount of the capacity of your cooling system. (For example, a 10-quart system needs 5 quarts of antifreeze.)

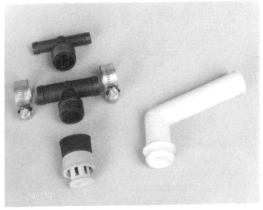

Flushing fitting kit—This takes only a couple of minutes to install and takes the work out of flushing the cooling system.

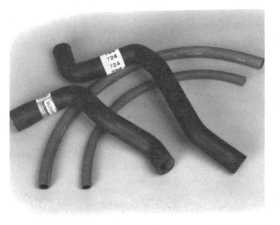

Radiator and heater hoses—Replace them every 2 years and reduce the risk of being stranded on the highway. Your auto parts store will help you get the correct size.

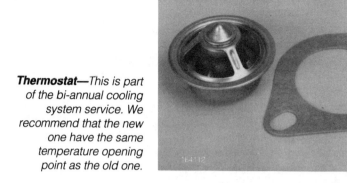

Thermostat—*This is part of the bi-annual cooling system service. We recommend that the new one have the same temperature opening point as the old one.*

Brake fluid—*Make sure it's the same type that's already in your brake system. DOT Type 3 is the most common, although some late model cars use DOT Type 4. Check your Owner's Manual.*

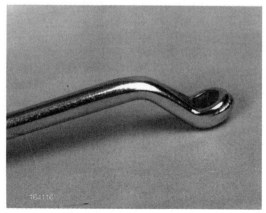

Brake bleeder wrench—*This tool won't round off the corners of the bleeder valve like a conventional wrench will.*

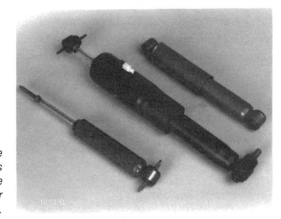

Shock absorbers—*See Section 10 for guidelines on selecting the right type of shock absorber for your driving and your vehicle.*

WD-40—*Use it to lubricate rubber bushings, penetrate rusted threads, or as a light-duty solvent and lubricant.*

Rust penetrant—*This is a serious, single-purpose chemical designed to attack heavy rust. It's a must for busting loose rusty nuts and bolts. Consider carrying a small can in your trunk to free up rusted lug nuts.*

Brake cleaner—*There's no safe substitute cleaner for brake work. Brake cleaner degreases as it cleans and doesn't leave an oil film on brake rotors and drums.*

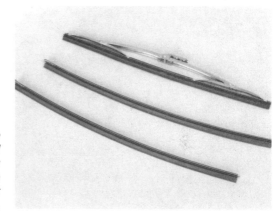

Windshield wiper blade inserts—*Take your old inserts with you when you buy new ones to make sure you get the correct size and type.*

White lithium grease—*This is a good multi-purpose lubricant for such things as door, hood, and trunk hinges, hood and trunk latch mechanisms.*

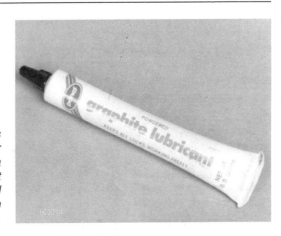

Graphite lubricant—This is used to lubricate door and trunk locks. It's in a dry powder form so it won't attract dust nor will it get gummy in cold weather.

Stainless stick lubricant—This is a clear, wax-like lubricant that won't stain clothes. It's perfect for lubricating door strikers that you can brush against getting into a vehicle.

Section 3:
Engine Oil and Filter Change

WHY FREQUENT OIL CHANGES ARE CRITICALLY IMPORTANT

Nothing contributes as much to premature engine failure as dirty engine oil. In addition to lubricating the contact surfaces, oil attracts and holds microscopic dirt and metal particles. These come from piston rings, cylinders, camshafts, and lifters as they wear down, as well as from dirty combustion by-products. When changed regularly, oil carries these particles out of the engine so they can't harm it. When the oil isn't changed, particles continue to build up until the entire mess becomes a very effective grinding paste! But don't take our word for it—look at what dirty oil can do to an engine.

Lube, Oil, & Chassis Service

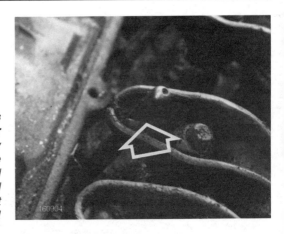

This pushrod ground its way through the rocker arm with the help of filthy engine oil. This extreme example of neglected service had only three oil changes in its rather short 70,000-mile life!

This photo should help you appreciate more fully our recommendation in Section 1 that you change oil and oil filter every 3,000 miles. Since do-it-yourselfers don't have to pay a labor charge, the cost is cheap and the benefit enormous. We do not intend to imply that following the manufacturer's recommendation for longer intervals will cause this type of damage. It won't. But if you follow our recommendation for more frequent changes, you can reasonably expect tens of thousands of added miles of reliable engine performance.

HOW TO SELECT THE BEST OIL FOR YOUR ENGINE

We recommend you use oil with an API (American Petroleum Institute) grade of SG—the best available today. These are compounded to cover virtually all driving conditions and are recommended by new-car manufacturers. Also, select the multigrade viscosity range that's correct for the prevailing ambient seasonal temperature in your locale. Here are recommendations that are typical of most manufacturers:

■ **Moderate climate** (ambient temperature never less than 0°F)—10W-30 or 10W-40.

■ **Hot climate** (ambient temperature never less than 50°F)—20W-40 or 20W-50.

■ **Cold climate** (ambient temperature never above 50°F with frequent freezing)—5W-30.

API grade and viscosity information is shown on the label on bottles and on the lid on cans. Check your Owner's Manual for grade and viscosity recommendations.

For maximum protection, we recommend you choose the widest viscosity range. In other words, we prefer a 20W-50 to 20W-40.

Lube, Oil, & Chassis Service

IS SYNTHETIC OIL RIGHT FOR YOUR ENGINE?

Synthetic oils—which use base stocks that are manufactured by organic reactions rather than refined from petroleum crude oil—have maintained a low profile with the general public for a couple of decades. But over the past few years, synthetic oils have become widely available and more reasonably priced.

While not the first synthetic oil, Mobil One may well be the best known. It is available in two viscosity ranges. Excellent synthetic oil is also available from Quaker State and other manufacturers.

Should you use synthetic oil in your engine's crankcase? Synthetic oils offer significant advantages over petroleum-based oils, but at a cost that is still significantly higher than petroleum-based oil.

The main advantage of synthetic oils is their high viscosity index—their ability to flow the same at both low and high temperatures. While the viscosity grades of synthetic oils are similar to those of premium multi-viscosity petroleum oils (i.e., 15W-50), there is more to the story than the numbers reveal.

Multigrade petroleum oils achieve a high viscosity index by modifying the molecules of the base oil with various additives. Thus, a 15W grade oil (which must pass a test to flow at -20°C (-4°F)) has its structure modified so that it meets the standards of a 50 grade oil at 100°C (212°F). The problem is that the additives that raise the viscosity index can break down at prolonged high temperatures or in the presence of normal crankcase contaminants. When this happens, the oil can either revert to its base viscosity or turn into a heavy goo. Either result can have disastrous effects on your engine.

The structure of a synthetic oil is engineered from the beginning to have a high viscosity index—much higher, in fact, than is possible for a petroleum oil. And the viscosity of a synthetic oil remains stable at much higher temperatures. (If you own a turbocharged car, you have all the reason you need to make the investment in a change to synthetic oil.) What this means is that a 15W-50 synthetic oil retains its 50-weight characteristics at temperatures far above the 100°C (212°F) standard measurement while also demonstrating no tendency to revert to a different viscosity.

Tests performed by an automobile manufacturer in the early '70's demonstrated that the lubricating characteristics of a particular synthetic oil remained consistent in over 100,000 miles of typical use in a then-current automobile.

But before you get the idea of bolting your hood closed, be aware that for these tests, the oil filter was changed at 5,000-mile intervals and detergent additive packages were added when chemical testing indicated a deterioration. Remember, an oil does much more than lubricate. Its cleaning and corrosion-protection duties require efficient filters and fresh additives. In other words, don't try this at home, kids!

As in deciding whether or not to use over-the-counter oil additives, your decision to use a synthetic oil should be based on how you use your vehicle. The first consideration should be temperature. If you have to start your engine on sub-zero mornings, nothing will flow as well as a synthetic oil. On the other end of the thermometer, if you frequently require your engine to work hard at high rpm (or if you have a turbo), a synthetic oil will hold up better than a petroleum-based oil. If you want to run your oil changes as long as your Owner's Manual recommends (which is a lot longer than we are comfortable with), a synthetic oil will give you added peace of mind.

And don't be concerned about switching to a synthetic oil if your vehicle has a few miles on the odometer. Unless you're using an overly high viscosity oil to compensate for bad gaskets or worn parts, you'll experience no adverse effects with a change to synthetic oil.

Synthetic oils do cost more, but you get better performance. Just as you did when you bought your vehicle, you must decide whether you need all the performance you can get.

WHAT OIL ADDITIVES CAN—AND CANNOT—DO

If you use any type of motor oil other than single-weight non-detergent, you already use oil additives, because that's the way detergent oil is compounded. Without additives, motor oil couldn't handle its demanding job in today's automotive engines. It must lubricate—keep the moving engine parts from touching—in all conditions, from a twenty-below winter day when the engine first starts, to a summer haul on the Interstate when underhood temperatures exceed 200°F. On top of that, it has to cool and seal the piston rings and cylinder walls, prevent deposits and varnishes from building up in the engine, and prevent corrosion.

Engine manufacturers and oil producers have developed over twenty-five tests an engine oil must pass to ensure that it can live up to all those demands. Non-detergent oils can't pass more than one of those tests!

With all those additives already in motor oil, why add more? It depends on how you use your vehicle. To help you determine what additives, if any, you should consider, let's examine additives in general and the jobs they do. Oil additives can be placed in two categories—detergents and viscosity index improvers.

Detergents keep varnishes and deposits from forming in your engine and actually can remove some deposits that may have already formed. Detergents also help prevent corrosion by neutralizing acids that build up in your engine and oil. Detergents are necessary because of the by-products of combustion that find their way into the oil and because of the wide range of temperatures in which engines operate.

If your oil is always at an optimum temperature of about 230°F, most of these by-products are carried off by the crankcase ventilation system while the others remain benignly suspended in the oil until you drain it. At high engine temperatures, however, these by-products can form varnishes and deposits that create friction and wear. At low oil temperature, below 200°F, water from normal condensation and from combustion can combine with these by-products to form acids which can eat into engine internals. Clearly, detergents are essential to the long life of your engine.

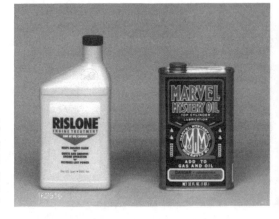

Detergent additives, such as venerable old Rislone and Marvel Mystery Oil, are easy to identify by such claims as "cleans carbon deposits and tunes."

Viscosity index improvers permit oil to do its job over a wide range of temperatures. Viscosity is the thickness of oil—its resistance to flow. The higher the number, the higher the viscosity. A 40-weight oil is thicker than a 20-weight oil.

Since an oil's viscosity decreases with temperature (it gets thinner when it gets hotter), oil viscosity is determined at specified temperatures. "W" (Winter) grade oils are measured at temperatures from -5°C to -30°C

(23°F to -22°F). All oils are also measured at 100°C (212°F).

The viscosity requirements of an engine oil are complex. The thinnest oil that still maintains sufficient film strength to keep engine parts from touching is desirable because of its low friction and ability to flow quickly when the engine is first started. But an oil that flows well at -20°F won't maintain its film strength during a long highway drive. And that's the reason for viscosity index improvers.

The viscosity index measures how much the oil thins out with increased temperature—the higher the viscosity index, the less the change. Viscosity index improvers allowed formulation of the first multi-grade oils, such as 10W-30, which means the oil flows like 10W oil at low temperatures and behaves like a 30W oil at 100°C (212°F). Improvements in chemistry over the years have brought us the 10W-40 and 15W-50 oil to provide the best of all worlds—almost.

Viscosity index improvers include STP, Wynn's, and dozens more. *Most also contain some detergent additives. Look for such claims as "Improves oil pressure and viscosity at high temperature."*

Detergents and viscosity index improvers are chemicals, and like all chemicals are subject to change in their properties—they can get used up.

In a vehicle used for short commutes in winter, detergents blended in the oil can be overloaded by the amount of combustion by-products they must deal with and the fact that the oil temperature is never high enough to allow them to work most efficiently. In the same engine during a hot summer trip at highway speeds, oil temperatures can become high enough to break down chemical additives and cause the oil to thicken, while the constant shearing of oil molecules at high engine speeds will permanently thin the oil to a lower viscosity.

Over-the-counter oil additives can help. If most of your driving consists of short around-town trips in which the oil never has a chance to get up to operating temperature, a detergent additive could help fight acids and varnish. On the other hand, if your engine is always working hard at high temperatures and high speeds, a viscosity index improver can help the oil maintain its designed viscosity.

But remember, dumping a can of additive into your engine's crankcase won't replace a needed oil change any more than it will repair worn rings or valve guides. Oil additives are not magic cures, but they can play a part in keeping your engine running well and long.

HOW TO BUY THE RIGHT OIL FILTER FOR YOUR ENGINE

The best piece of advice we can give you about buying oil filters is "buy quality." In this case quality doesn't mean high cost. The best and most reputable brands of oil filters are actually reasonably priced.

All of the filters shown are high quality. Just as important, they are all reasonably priced and readily available. In fact, the three brands shown were purchased at the same auto parts store.

We suggest that you avoid super-bargain oil filters—the kind with a brand name you've never heard of and a whopping savings of two whole dollars! Many such bargain filters are poorly made and use cheap paper as a filter element. Not only do they not filter effectively, they might actually restrict oil flow and cause major engine damage!

Most auto parts stores hang filter application directories or "catalogs" near the oil filter display shelves. To find the filter your engine needs, simply find the make, model, year, and engine type for your vehicle in the catalog and there's the filter number. Occasionally, two numbers will be listed—one for normal service and another for heavy duty. The heavy-duty filter is usually longer than the standard one. So, before buying the larger filter make sure it will fit

Lube, Oil, & Chassis Service

your engine and you have clearance to install and remove it. Often, the smaller filter is required for clearance on some vehicles.

The longer heavy-duty filter fits the same engine as the shorter one. However, the longer filter may not fit on some vehicles using the same engine because of limited space between the engine and the chassis.

LOVE YOUR PLANET: DISPOSE OF OLD OIL PROPERLY

Before you begin an oil change, plan how you're going to dispose of the old oil safely and responsibly. Used motor oil is a hazardous substance, so it must be handled and disposed of carefully. Don't put old oil in with your trash. Don't pour it on the ground. Don't pour it down the sewer or a storm drain. You don't want old oil to end up in your ground water!

Most service stations will accept your used oil. However, there may be a slight charge. Many community recycling centers are equipped to handle old oil. You should find them listed near the front of your community telephone book. Or, check the telephone white pages for your state's Bureau of Weights and Measures or the local EPA office and ask for a listing of approved disposal sites.

HOW TO CHECK ENGINE OIL LEVEL AND CONDITION

We strongly recommend you check your oil level every time you fill up your tank. This is very important on long trips at sustained highway speeds when you fill the tank a couple of times each day. As an absolute minimum in very light driving, check engine oil level and condition at least once a month. (We suspect that most readers of this book know how to check the oil level. But the procedure may be useful for training other family members.)

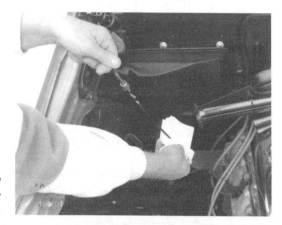

Pull out the dipstick and wipe it with a clean rag or paper towel.

Then, insert the dipstick until its collar contacts the tube, pull it out again, and compare the oil level against the marks on the tip of the dipstick.

The oil level should be between the upper and lower marks on the dipstick. *The difference between the marks is 1 quart. This engine is about 1 quart low.*

To add oil, first remove the oil filler cap. *In most cases the filler cap is located on the valve cover or cam cover, and is removed by turning it a quarter of a turn counterclockwise.*

Insert a funnel in the oil filler hole. *This makes it easy to add oil without spilling or dripping it onto the engine or the exhaust system.*

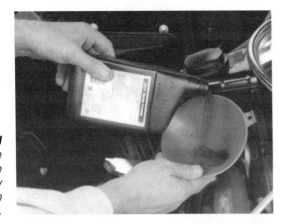

Add oil to correct the oil level. Even if you think the engine might be a couple of quarts low, add only one quart and then recheck the level.

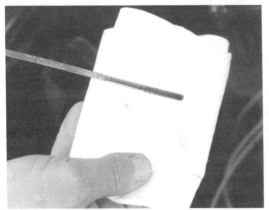

After adding oil, wait a few minutes for the new oil to drain down into the crankcase, then recheck the level to make sure it's between the marks. If it's still lower than the bottom mark, add another quart of oil and recheck again. The level shown here is okay and no more oil needs to be added.

Check the gasket in the oil filler cap to make sure it seals well and doesn't allow oil fumes to escape. If the seal is worn or damaged, replace the cap as soon as possible.

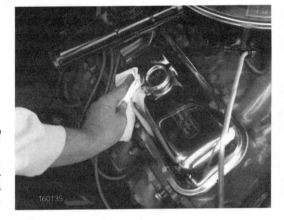

Install the filler cap and wipe up any spilled oil, *particularly any that's gotten onto the exhaust manifold. Be careful—it may be hot!*

Even a healthy engine will use a little oil, so don't worry if you have to add a quart or two between oil changes. However, if you have to add more than a quart every 1,000 miles, something's not right.

PRO TIP: Causes of High Oil Consumption

High oil consumption can be caused by any one of a number of things, such as worn valve guides or seals, worn piston rings and cylinder bores, or leakage. The causes for high oil consumption are shown in the Quick-Check Table below, along with suggested corrections and repairs.

Possible Cause	Correction
Incorrect reading on dipstick.	Check oil with vehicle level and allow adequate drain-down time.
External oil leaks.	Tighten bolts and/or replace gaskets and seals as necessary.
Incorrect oil viscosity.	Use recommended viscosity for prevailing temperature. See your Owner's Manual.
Continuous high-speed driving and/or severe usage.	Increased oil consumption is normal under these conditions.
Crankcase ventilation or PCV system malfunction.	Check PCV system and clean or replace PCV valves and hoses as necessary.
Piston rings not seated in new or rebuilt engine.	Allow adequate time for rings to seat (1,000+ miles).
Valve guides and/or valve stem seals worn, or seals missing.	Check compression. Repair or rebuild cylinder head(s).
Broken or worn piston rings.	Replace broken or worn rings.

OIL CONDITION TELLS A STORY

Every time you check oil level, also look closely at the dipstick to see the condition of the oil. It can indicate an existing problem or help you spot impending engine trouble before it leads to serious damage. New oil will be clear amber, and it will darken to a golden-brown in the first few hundred miles of normal use in a good engine.

If you notice any of the following conditions while you're checking the oil, your vehicle is in need of immediate attention:

- **Very dark oil,** despite regular oil changes, may indicate that combustion products are entering the crankcase because of worn or damaged cylinders and/or piston rings.

- **Frothy or milky oil** is a sign that engine coolant may be entering the oil through a leak in a cylinder head gasket or the engine block.

- **Shiny particles in the oil** may indicate significant internal wear or damage.

If possible, check the level when the engine is cold, or has been shut off for 5 minutes. This allows oil to drain back to the pan from the top of the engine and ensures an accurate reading.

And while you're checking the engine oil, check the gasket in the oil filler cap to make sure it seals well. A poorly sealed cap allows oil fumes to escape rather than be recycled through the PCV system. This is bad from an emissions standpoint, and the fumes will coat the engine compartment with a fine oily film that attracts dirt. This condition can quickly turn your engine into a grease ball.

PRO TIP: Make Sure Your Engine Doesn't Become a Trash Bin

Those convenient plastic oil bottles that replaced cans a couple of years ago have a downside. The foil seal that some oil companies use on the neck can wind up in the engine if you don't completely remove it. Also, the little plastic lockring that stays on the neck when the cap is unscrewed can fall into the engine, as can foil or plastic cap liners that stick to the neck of the bottle rather than stay in the cap.

And if you are using a funnel to direct oil into the engine, make sure the funnel is clean both inside and out before sticking it into the oil fill opening.

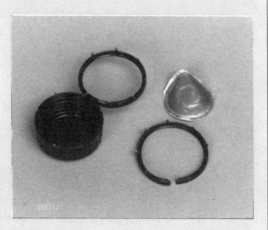

Remove foil seals and lock rings from oil bottles before pouring oil into the engine. If these little pieces wind up inside your engine they can block oil passages.

HOW TO CHANGE ENGINE OIL AND FILTER

It's best to drain the oil when the engine is at normal operating temperature, just after it has been run. Warm oil drains more easily, and the contaminants will still be suspended in it.

For an oil change you will need:

■ The necessary amount of oil in the correct grade and viscosity.

■ New oil filter.

■ New sealing washer for the drain plug.

■ A drain-and-store container or a 6-quart drain pan and a sealable container large enough to hold the old oil.

■ An oil filter wrench.

■ A box-end wrench for the drain plug.

■ A funnel.

■ A fender cover.

■ Lots of rags and newspapers.

■ A can opener or oil can spout (for oil in cans).

If your vehicle is extremely low, you will also need:

■ A jack, jack stands, and wheel chocks.

■ Eye protection—For when you are crawling under the vehicle. (Exhaust systems develop metal "dandruff" that can injure your eyes.)

PRO TIP: How to Remove a Stubborn Oil Filter

If you've changed more than a couple of oil filters you have probably encountered one that you were sure wouldn't come off. They always do, however, but usually with a great deal of effort and mess.

The time-honored method of driving a large screwdriver through the filter and using it as a handle almost always works—although we have seen that method fail in at least one case. The screwdriver method usually results in a mess as oil pours out the sides of the filter when it's first punctured.

For the cleanest way to remove a stubborn filter, fold a strip of sandpaper in two so the abrasive faces out on both sides. Then, wrap the sandpaper around the filter and install a strap-type filter wrench over it. The sandpaper will grip both the filter and the filter wrench, preventing them from slipping, allowing you to break the filter loose.

Get a grip on a stubborn oil filter with sandpaper folded so there is abrasive on both sides. This will grip the filter and the wrench and prevent the wrench from slipping.

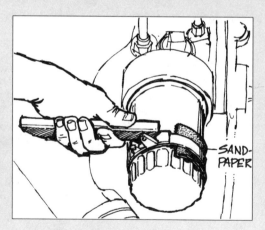

Lube, Oil, & Chassis Service

Pro Tip: Eliminating the Mess With Inverted Filters

Inverted oil filters—those that are installed with the open end facing down—can make a real mess of your engine when you remove them and trapped oil runs down the block and onto anything under the filter.

To reduce the amount of oil in the filter—by letting it drain out through the engine—puncture the top of the filter with a screwdriver or punch to ventilate it. This allows most of the oil to drain out of the filter and reduces the mess when you remove it.

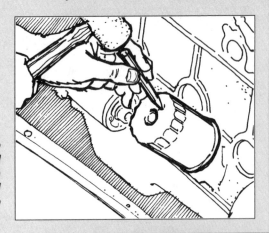

Punch a hole in the top of an inverted filter to allow air in which will help the oil drain back into the engine.

After the engine has reached operating temperature, shut it off, and remove the oil filler cap. This allows air to enter the crankcase and speed up drainage.

Drain the crankcase.
Loosen the plug with a wrench but remove it by hand so you won't drop it into the drain pan. After the oil has drained, don't install the drain plug until you've removed the filter. "Suction" created by the filter can hold old oil in the passages and keep it from draining until the "suction" is broken.

Position the drain pan under the oil filter and remove the filter. Loosen it one-half turn with a filter wrench, and spin it off by hand. Watch out, it may be hot. Keep the open end of the filter up to minimize oil drips.

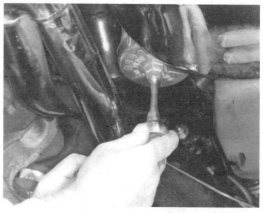

Clean the filter-mounting surface. Wipe off old oil and grime. Remove the oil filter gasket if it's stuck to the engine. Failure to do this is guaranteed to result in a major oil leak when the new filter is installed.

PRO TIP: Let's Keep It Clean

Horizontal and angled oil filters are difficult to remove without making a mess, particularly if they are mounted above hoses, fluid lines, wires, or brackets.

If you have this sort of situation in your vehicle, cover any hoses or parts beneath the oil filter with kitchen plastic wrap before you unscrew the filter. The plastic will direct spilled oil down into the drip pan, and when you're through just remove the plastic from the protected and clean hoses, lines, wires, and brackets.

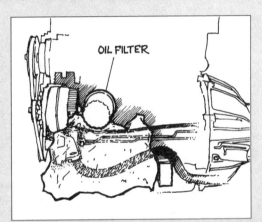

Plastic kitchen wrap keeps oil off of hoses, wires, or any parts that are located beneath a side-mounted oil filter.

Oil the gasket on the new filter. Coat the new filter gasket lightly with fresh engine oil.

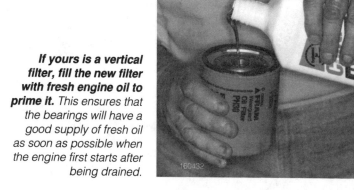

If yours is a vertical filter, fill the new filter with fresh engine oil to prime it. *This ensures that the bearings will have a good supply of fresh oil as soon as possible when the engine first starts after being drained.*

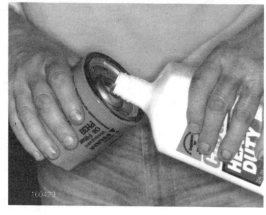

If the filter is angled, hold in the installed position *and fill it with fresh oil for a complete prime.*

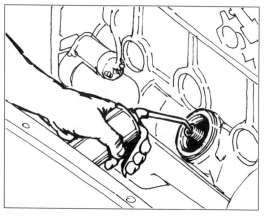

If yours is an angled or horizontal filter, *inject about five squirts of fresh engine oil into the inlet in the filter mounting base on the engine. This ensures that the oil pump is primed and ready to supply fresh oil to the bearings as soon as possible when the engine first starts.*

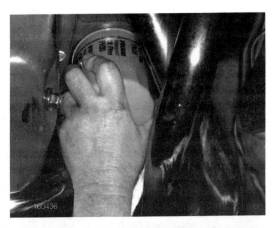

Install the new filter by hand. *If there are instructions on the filter, tighten it as specified. If there are no instructions, tighten the filter 3/4 turn more after the gasket has made contact with the engine.*

Install the drain plug with a new sealing washer. *Tighten the plug firmly but not so much you crack the washer, or worse, strip the threads in the pan. Even a slight nick or crack in the washer will create an annoying oil leak.*

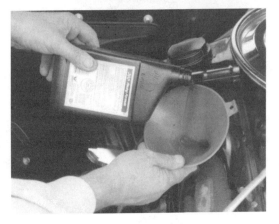

Fill the crankcase. *With the aid of a funnel, pour the required number of quarts of oil in through the filler opening, and install the oil filler cap.*

PRO TIP: A Matter of Prime Importance

You should prime the new filter before starting the engine to ensure there is good oil pressure as soon as the engine starts. To do this, you must first disable the ignition to prevent the engine from starting.

As much sense as this step makes, it's rarely ever done by service stations, dealerships, or even the quick-lube pros. Granted, it takes a few minutes more to do, but it will pay off in long-term dividends in the form of thousands of additional miles from your engine.

For conventional ignition, unplug the primary coil wire from the distributor cap to disable the ignition.

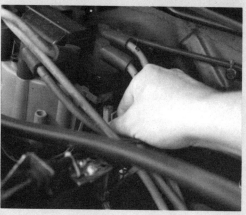

For electronic ignition, disconnect the primary wire from the control box to prevent the engine from starting.

Crank the engine with the starter until the oil light goes out *(or the needle rises if you have a gauge). The filter is primed and you now have oil pressure.*

Reconnect the coil (or the primary wire), *to restore ignition function. Now you can start the engine with the oil system fully primed.*

Start the engine and check for leaks. *Pay particular attention to the drain plug and the base of the filter. If the filter is leaking, give it another quarter turn.*

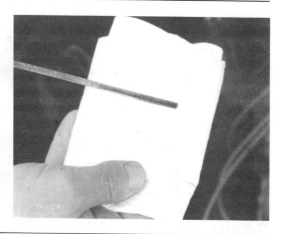

Check and correct the oil level. Stop the engine, and let it sit several minutes to allow the oil to drain back to the crankcase. Check the oil level at the dipstick. Add oil only if the level is below the bottom or ADD mark.

PRO TIP: Easy Does It for Cold-Weather Warm-Ups

Take your time during cold-weather warm-ups, and don't race the engine. Let the fast-idle system on the carburetor or fuel injection handle engine speed.

Cold, stiff oil just doesn't want to move very fast. When you rev the engine you increase oil pressure and force oil through the filter, among other places. This can result in a split crimp seam at the base of the filter. This, of course, results in loss of oil and oil pressure with possible damage to the engine. So be patient and let the engine—and the oil—warm up slowly.

Lube, Oil, & Chassis Service

PRO TIP: One Solution for Slow Oil Pressure Rise

If you notice that your oil pressure light is staying on longer than usual after you first start the engine in the morning, check to make sure the oil level is correct. If it's okay, you still may not be facing a rebuild in the near future.

The problem could be caused by a jammed anti-drainback valve in the filter. This valve keeps the filter full when the engine is shut off by preventing the oil from draining back into the pan. The idea here is to ensure that the oil pump doesn't first have to fill the filter before it starts supplying oil to the bearings. Hard particles, such as a piece of carbon or a sand grain, could be holding the valve open, letting the oil drain back into the pan when the engine sits for several hours.

So, if everything else is normal when the long oil light starts to occur, have the oil and filter changed and the problem just may disappear.

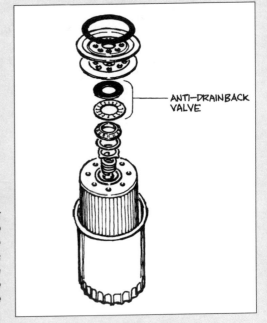

ANTI–DRAINBACK VALVE

The anti-drainback valve keeps oil in the engine when the engine is shut off. This ensures that there is an adequate supply to the bearings when the engine is started.

Section 4:

Steering and Suspension

HOW TO INSPECT AND LUBE STEERING AND SUSPENSION JOINTS

You should inspect the underside of your vehicle for signs of wear, damage, or leakage every time you change the oil. If you have a vehicle that you drive off-road, you should hose off and inspect the front suspension after every trip. Pay particular attention for damage to:

- Steering gearbox and steering column joints.

- Steering linkage ball joints.

- Suspension control arm ball joints.

- Front axle CV (constant velocity) joint dust boots (front-wheel-drive and four-wheel-drive models).

Lube, Oil, & Chassis Service

If you frequently drive in deep water, it's a good idea to lubricate ball joints and steering joints after every trip. If your vehicle doesn't have grease fittings—as is the case with many late-model cars and trucks—you'll have to install them before you can grease the joints. (See *How to Install grease fittings in suspension joints,* page 54.)

Suspension and chassis repairs usually require special tools and wheel alignment, so it's best to leave these repairs to a competent professional.

To inspect and lube the steering joints you don't need much:

- A jack, two jack stands, and wheel chocks.
- A grease gun.
- Eye protection.

Raise and support the front end, making sure it's safely supported and not likely to fall. Then, unlock the steering column so you can turn the front wheels from side to side.

Check steering and suspension boots for cracks and rips by extending and squeezing them. The boots keep water and dirt out of the joints and hold grease in. When a boot is damaged, the joint is no longer protected and can wear out rapidly. For CV joints, replace bad boots as soon as you find them (see page 56).

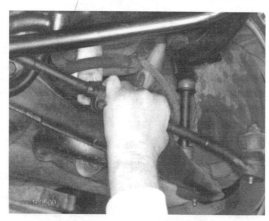

Check the steering gearbox and linkage for looseness, damage, and signs of leakage. Inspect all steering links for looseness by grabbing and shaking each one individually. Look for loose and missing parts, like cotter pins, washers, and nuts.

Check the ball joints on the steering linkage for looseness, damaged dust seals, and signs of leakage. Inspect the suspension ball joints for the same conditions. Test them for looseness by gripping the top and bottom of each tire and shaking the wheel, listening and feeling for "clunks."

Control arms take a tremendous pounding, so check them for cracks, damage, and road-salt corrosion. Failure of a control arm results in loss of control of the vehicle. So, inspect the arms regularly, and flush off dirt and road salt with high-pressure water. Have damaged arms replaced as soon as you spot them.

Lubricate the ball joints.
Clean the grease fitting, and push the end of the grease gun nozzle onto it. Pump the gun slowly until the dust seal just starts to bulge. Then, remove the nozzle, and wipe excess grease off of the fitting.

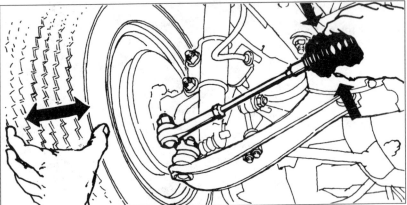

On front-wheel-drive cars, feel for looseness in the steering joints by squeezing the boot and turning the wheels from side to side. If you feel any play, replace the joints as soon as possible. Otherwise, your front tires will wear out prematurely.

PRO TIP: Bump Stops Tell the Story

The rubber bump stops on your suspension are excellent indicators of spring and shock absorber wear and damage. The bump stops, which prevent metal-to-metal contact between the suspension and frame, should be inspected when you inspect the rest of the suspension.

Harsh impact causes cuts on the bump stops, and constant rubbing causes scuffing. If you find either of these conditions, inspect the shocks (page 139) and check the springs for sag (page 62). Once you've taken care of the problem, replace the bump stops.

Damaged bump stops are an indication that the shocks and springs should be checked.

Lube, Oil, & Chassis Service

PRO TIP: How to Install Grease Fittings in Suspension Joints

Front suspension ball joints and steering joints are lubricated with grease. On many cars and trucks, the joints are filled with grease and sealed with a screw-in plug at the factory, and don't need to be lubricated in normal use—so say the manufacturers.

But dirt and water can enter the ball joints, particularly if the vehicle is frequently driven in heavy rain or through deep water, mud, or snow. If you use your vehicle for this kind of driving, you should install grease fittings on the suspension and steering joints the first time you inspect the front suspension, and grease the joints weekly during continuous severe use.

Like many owners, we feel that periodic greasing of suspension and steering joints can't do any harm, and in fact probably contributes to longer life for these hard-working parts, even when they are not subjected to severe service. For this reason, we recommend the installation of grease fittings in joints that are equipped to take them.

There are many types of grease fittings, but most vehicles use only a few types. The most common of these are either straight or angled—45 degrees. Access to the joint is what determines the type of fitting that's needed. You'll have to determine which ones you need.

Make sure you have the correct thread size and type—either metric or American. Remove a plug from one of the joints and have the parts counterman where you buy the fittings match them to the plug.

The most common types of grease fittings—straight and 45 degrees. Access to the fitting determines the type you need. Also check to see if you need metric or American.

Remove the plugs from the joints. Then, compare the threads on the plug to those on the grease fitting to make sure they are the same.

Install the new grease fitting. Make certain it's positioned so the grease gun nozzle will fit on it.

HOW TO REPLACE CV-JOINT BOOTS

Constant velocity (CV) joints are tough and are designed to last the life of the vehicle. However, the boots that protect CV joints are rather fragile by comparison. They are easily torn and cracked, allowing dirt and water to get into the joint and chew it up. It's no exaggeration to say that damaged CV joint boots are the largest single cause of premature CV joint wear and failure.

With replacement costs of CV joints running $500 to $700, keeping the joints well protected becomes a priority item.

The cost of having just the original-equipment type boots replaced is also substantial, because it involves most of the same labor required to replace CV joints. OEM-type boots are a one-piece design, and require full disassembly of the CV joint in order to slip them over the axle.

However, you can do a first-rate job yourself, without special tools, and save the labor costs by replacing damaged CV joint boots with new split boots. Split boots are available for almost all FWD and 4WD vehicles with front axle CV joints.

There are several types of split boots available. Split boots are easy to install, because you do not have to disassemble the axle. Installed properly, split boots should be as durable as original equipment boots. The procedure shown features the "Quick Boot" brand split boot. Its design allows you to seal it completely during installation so dirt and moisture cannot get into the joint.

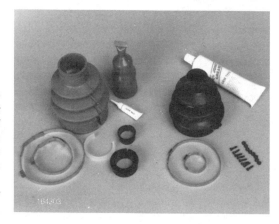

The Quick Boot on the left lets you seal it completely so dirt and moisture cannot get into the joint. The split boot on the right uses screws to hold the split together. Both types are easy to install.

To install split boots, you'll have to work under the vehicle, so raise and support the front end on frame stands so it can't fall. Make sure the parking brake is applied and the wheels are securely chocked. And don't forget to wear eye protection.

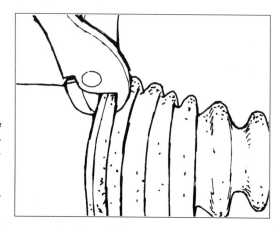

Cut the old boot off of the axle. Side cutters or tin snips will usually work to cut the old band. However, on GM joints a chisel works best to cut the band.

Clean and repack the CV joint. *If there is no grit in the joint, just clean the axle and clamping area. If the joint is dirty, use an aerosol type cleaner to remove old grease, dirt, and moisture. Then pack the joint with the special CV grease that comes in the boot kit.*

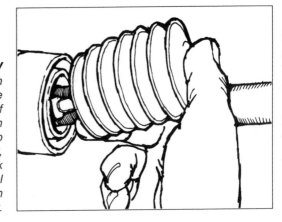

Wrap the new boot around the shaft. *Don't slide it into position over the large flange on the differential just yet.*

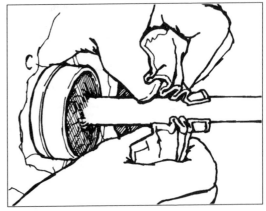

Apply solvent to the female or U-shaped side of the seam. *Also apply a bead around the inside of the large end of the boot to act as a gasket. Wipe any solvent off of the outside of the boot.*

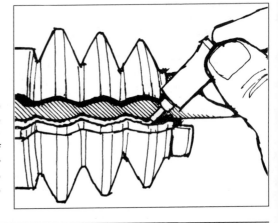

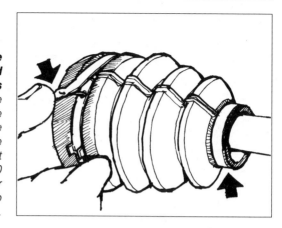

Immediately install the boot over the flange and press the edges together. Install the permanent clamp on the large end and the temporary clamp on the small end. Hold the boot together for about 60 seconds then let it sit for at least 10 minutes to thoroughly bond.

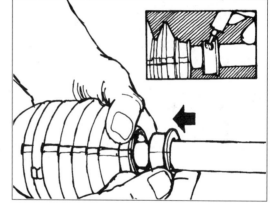

Apply solvent to the adapter for the small end. The solvent must go all around the outside of the adapter. Insert the adapter into the boot, and install the clamp.

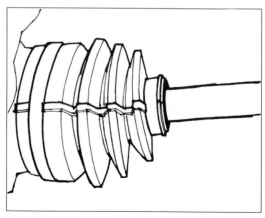

Allow at least 20 minutes for the seam and adapter to fully bond. Inspect the boot to make sure it's correctly installed and thoroughly sealed.

PRO TIP: Bad Suspension Bushings Are Often the Cause of Poor Handling and Ride

To ensure correct ride and handling, it's not enough to replace the shocks, ball joints, tie-rod ends, steering arm, idler arm, and have the front end aligned. A total "front-end job" is *not* complete until the rubber suspension bushings have been checked and bad ones replaced. When bushings wear out (or deteriorate because of ozone attack), there's nothing you can do to correct ride and handling problems until they are replaced. This is true for the rear suspension as well as the front.

Bushing replacement is a simple, straightforward job—no rocket science here. But, it's a lot of hard work that will probably take a full weekend of your time, plus some help from a full-size friend. You will need a good shop manual for this job, plus a service jack, jackstands, a large bench vise or a small press, and some hefty hand tools. If you don't already have the tools and equipment you need, you will probably be money ahead to have the work done by a suspension specialist.

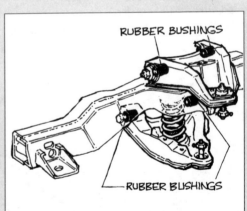

Rubber bushings in front suspension pivots are common in almost all cars and light trucks on the road today.

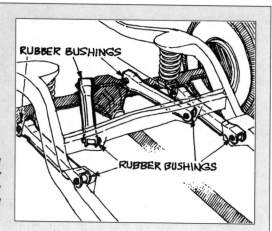

A typical coil-spring four-link rear suspension has eight rubber bushed connection points.

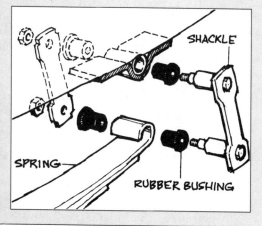

Leaf-spring rear suspension has rubber bushings on the shackle bolts. These are easy to replace, but the spring must be handled with great care and respect.

PRO TIP: How Do You Know When Your Springs or Torsion Bars Are Shot?

When front springs or torsion bars get weak and start to sag, almost everything in your front end suffers. Ball joints and steering linkage wear out faster, alignment is shot, tires wear quickly, and ride and handling are terrible. If you've experienced any of these conditions, or if your vehicle has logged a lot of hard miles, check your springs or torsion bars for sag. If your springs or torsion bars fail this simple inspection, they should be replaced.

■ Park on a level surface.

■ Measure the distance between the lower control arms and the frame—or subframe (A). The difference between the two should be no more than 1/4 inch.

■ Measure the distance from the outer end of the lower control arm to the ground (C). The difference between the two should be no more than 3/4 inch.

■ Measure the distance from the inner pivot of the lower control arm to the ground (B). The difference between the two should be no more than 3/4 inch.

■ Measure the distance from the lower edge of each end of the bumper to the ground (D). The difference between the two should be no more than 3/8 inch.

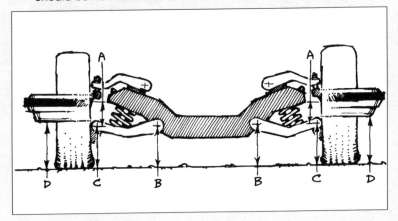

Section 5:

Transmission and Drivetrain

HOW TO CHECK AND CHANGE MANUAL TRANSMISSION OIL

Most manual transmissions use heavy oil to lubricate the gears and bearings. However, some (Honda Civic, Chevy Citation, Ford Tempo, and Mercury Topaz to name just a few) use engine oil or automatic transmission fluid. Thus, it's essential that you check your Owner's Manual to determine which type and how much oil your manual transmission requires.

Check manual transmission oil level at least once a year or every 15,000 miles. Check it more often if there are any leaks other than slight seepage around the seals.

If your transmission has a dipstick, check it as described in your Owner's Manual. If not, check the level (and change the oil when necessary) as described on the next page.

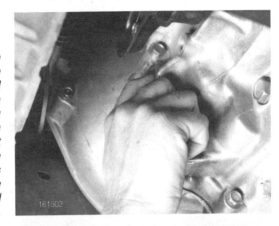

The oil level should be within 1/2 inch of the bottom of the fill/level hole. Remove the transmission fill/level plug and check the level with your finger. If you can't feel the oil, add the correct weight oil until it's up to the bottom of the hole. Then install and tighten the plug.

Remove the drain plug to change the oil. When the old oil has drained, install and tighten the drain plug. Then fill the transmission with the correct grade of oil until the level reaches the bottom of the fill/level hole, and install and tighten the level plug.

HOW TO CHECK AUTOMATIC TRANSMISSION FLUID LEVEL AND CONDITION

Under normal driving conditions, you should check the level and condition of the automatic transmission fluid at every oil change.

To do this, you will need:

■ Automatic transmission fluid (if level is low). For Ford transmissions, use Type F ATF. For GM, Chrysler, and most others, use DEXRON II ATF.

■ Clean, lint-free paper.

Before checking the transmission fluid, warm the engine and transmission to normal operating temperature. (There are both HOT and COLD marks on most dipsticks, and it's okay to check the level cold. However, checking it with the fluid and transmission at operating temperature is the more accurate method.) Drive the car for at least 15 miles at highway speed. If the car has just been driven at sustained high speed, or in stop-and-go traffic, or in hot weather for an extensive period, you won't be able to obtain an accurate level reading. In such case, allow the transmission and fluid to cool for about a half hour before checking the level.

Park the car on a level surface, set the parking brake, start the engine, depress the foot brake, and move the selector lever through all of its positions, and then set it at PARK. Do not shut off the engine.

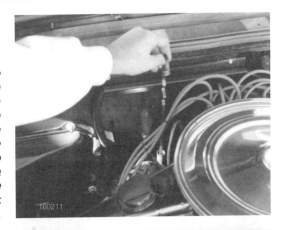

Clean the outside of the automatic transmission dipstick tube, *then remove and clean the dipstick with lint-free paper. Reinsert the dipstick all the way into the tube and wait a couple of seconds before pulling it out to check the level.*

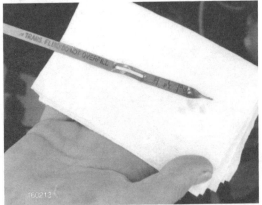

Compare the fluid level with the marks on the blade. *The difference between the L and H marks is about 1 pint (1/2 quart).*

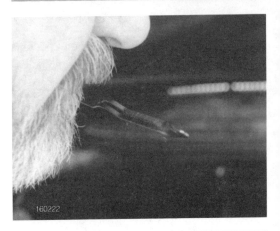

Inspect and smell the fluid. *It should be a clear, transparent red or green. If it's dark there may be internal damage, and the transmission may need rebuilding. If the fluid is milky, have the transmission cooler checked for a leak. See the Pro Tip on page 68 for more info.*

If the fluid is okay but the level is below the L mark, add 1 pint (1/2 quart) of transmission fluid through the dipstick tube, using a long-neck funnel.

Be careful not to overfill the transmission. Too much fluid is as bad as too little because it can cause the transmission to overheat.

After adding fluid, allow the engine to idle for several minutes, and then recheck the level. If it's still not between the marks, add another pint of transmission fluid. Never add more than 1 pint at a time until the level is correct.

Lube, Oil, & Chassis Service

PRO TIP: When to Replace Your Transmission Fluid

It's easy to tell when the fluid is low, and there's no trick to bringing it back up to its normal level. But how do you determine when the fluid needs replacing? By checking its color and odor. This check will also tell you about the condition of the transmission.

- If the fluid is clear, transparent red or green, and smells oily, it's okay. Wipe off the fluid onto a clean, white piece of paper and look for metal particles—a sure sign of wear and possible damage. If you find none, the transmission is okay.

- If the fluid is a dark reddish-brown, and has a distinctly burnt smell, a clutch/disc pack has experienced severe wear, due to slipping under heavy (abusive) use or a malfunction. Change the fluid and filter immediately. It has lost much of its protective properties and ability to lubricate. Check the fluid at every gas refill. If the dark burnt condition quickly comes back, the clutch/disc packs are slipping and the tranny probably needs rebuilding.

- If the fluid has a milky appearance there is probably antifreeze in the transmission. This is commonly caused by a leak in the transmission cooler located in the radiator. When you encounter this condition, repair the leak in the transmission cooler immediately, and replace the transmission fluid and filter. Recheck the fluid after 1,000 miles to make sure the coolant leak has been fixed.

Now the bad news. It's possible to get 5 to 20 thousand additional miles of service from a transmission that's been contaminated with coolant. However, we don't recommend that you count on it because irreversible damage has been done. Guidelines from the Hydramatic Division of GM call for removal, disassembly, cleaning, and replacement of all nonmetallic parts. There are a number of plastic seals in an automatic transmission that fail when contaminated with coolant. Also, the glue that attaches organic material to the plates in the clutch packs is dissolved by the coolant, permitting the clutch material to slough off.

Finally, it's virtually impossible to remove all contaminated fluid from the torque converter while it's still in the vehicle. And, the torque converter also has organic clutch material that's affected by the contamination. For this reason, the GM guidelines also call for replacement of the torque converter.

A transmission cooler leak can be tricky to fix, so we recommend you remove the radiator and have the cooler repaired by a radiator shop before operating a cleaned or rebuilt transmission.

PRO TIP: What to Do If Your Transmission is Too Full

If your automatic transmission is mistakenly overfilled, you must drain the excess fluid. Otherwise, the fluid will foam and the transmission will slip. This would be bad enough, but the slippage can cause the clutch/disc packs to wear and burn.

Unfortunately, most automatic transmissions don't have drain plugs. So, rather than remove the transmission pan and drain all the fluid, disconnect the lower transmission cooler line from the radiator and drain the excess fluid into a clean container. Then, reconnect the line and recheck the level. If you've drained too much, correct the level by adding some of the fluid you have just drained.

Fit a length of hose to the disconnected transmission line and drain fluid into a clean container. Start the engine and allow it to run for no more than 3 seconds. Reconnect the line and recheck the level as you would normally.

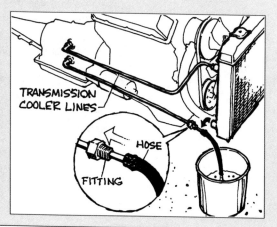

TRANSMISSION COOLER LINES

HOSE

FITTING

HOW TO DO A LEAK-FREE TRANSMISSION SERVICE FOR UNDER $30

Many automobile manufacturers recommend transmission filter and fluid change at intervals of 70,000 to 100,000 miles under normal driving conditions. This is probably okay for a car that has been treated right and not abused at any time during its life. We feel that 50,000-mile intervals are better.

Some truck manufacturers aren't quite so optimistic. GM, for example, recommends that the transmission fluid and filter in their full-size trucks be changed every 30,000 miles under normal conditions and at 15,000-mile intervals under severe use.

If you do a lot of stop-and-go driving or use your car or truck to tow a trailer, you're operating under severe driving conditions, and should check the transmission fluid level at least once a month, and replace the filter and fluid as often as every 12 months or 15,000 miles.

In spite of what you may have heard, changing the transmission fluid and filter is not a difficult job. We've provided some guidelines and tips from transmission service pros to make it as easy as possible.

Pay close attention to the condition of the old fluid and filter. They can help you diagnose causes for existing trouble or warn you about problems that may have just started. See the Pro Tip on page 68 for diagnosing fluid condition.

Make sure you have the correct filter, a new pan gasket, the correct amount and type of transmission fluid, and a large enough drain pan *before you start. Check your Owner's Manual for refill capacity and fluid type.*

Remove the drain plug and drain the oil. *Wait until oil flow slows to a few drips before removing the pan. Keep the pan level because there may still be quite a bit of oil in it.*

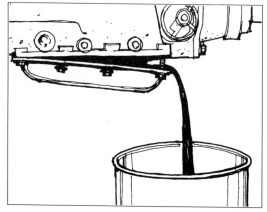

If there is no drain plug, loosen all the bolts a few turns and tilt the rear of the pan down to drain most of the fluid. *Then, remove the pan and drain the rest of the fluid. Check the fluid for metal particles and pieces of clutch material.*

Lube, Oil, & Chassis Service

Remove the old filter and any gasket—or O-ring. *Filter gaskets are very thin, about the same color as the valve body, and easy to overlook. Inspect the old filter for metal particles and pieces of clutch material—both signs of future trouble.*

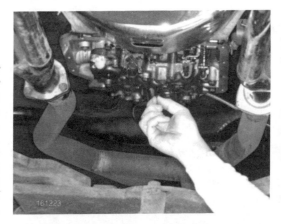

Install the new filter. *Be sure to include the new gasket (if there is one in your filter kit).*

Thoroughly clean the pan. *We recommend that you install an aftermarket drain plug in the pan if it doesn't have one. They are inexpensive and easy to install. Just follow the instructions that come with the plug. It makes subsequent service much easier and neater.*

Here's the secret of a leak-free transmission service. Dimple the mounting holes down with the ball end of a ball-peen hammer. Just making sure the rail is flat isn't good enough. You must actually dimple the holes so the entire rail—and not just the area around the hole—contacts the gasket.

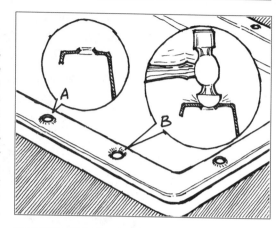

Remove all grease, oil, and dirt from the pan and transmission rails. Use denatured alcohol or lacquer thinner, and make sure the rails are perfectly clean and dry. This is essential to make sure the new gasket will stay in place.

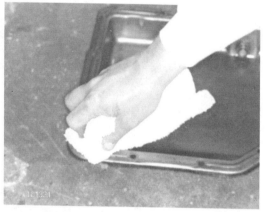

Set the new gasket on the pan rail and carefully position it against the transmission. **Do not use any sealer or cement on the gasket or any of the surfaces!** It acts like a lubricant and allows the gasket to slip out from between the pan and the transmission when the pan bolts are tightened.

Start all the bolts in before tightening any of them. *This helps ensure that the gasket is perfectly lined up.*

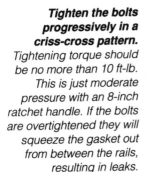

Tighten the bolts progressively in a criss-cross pattern. *Tightening torque should be no more than 10 ft-lb. This is just moderate pressure with an 8-inch ratchet handle. If the bolts are overtightened they will squeeze the gasket out from between the rails, resulting in leaks.*

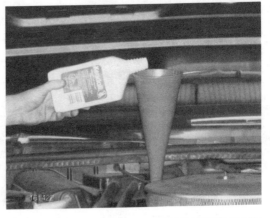

Fill the transmission with fresh fluid. *Use only as much as is recommended in your Owner's Manual. Check the level as described on page 65, and carefully make any final level adjustment with the transmission at operating temperature so you don't overfill it.*

HOW TO CHECK AND CHANGE REAR-DRIVE DIFFERENTIAL OIL

Rear-drive differentials are filled with heavy oil to lubricate the gears and bearings. However, recommended viscosities and capacities vary from one manufacturer to another, so it's important that you check your Owner's Manual to determine which type and how much oil your differential requires.

Check the differential oil level at least once a year or every 15,000 miles. Check it more often if there is any leakage other than slight seepage around the seals.

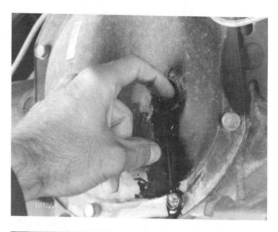

The oil level should be within 1/2 inch of the bottom of the fill/level hole. Remove the differential fill/level plug and check the level with your finger. If you can't feel the oil, add the correct weight oil until it's up to the bottom of the hole. Then install and tighten the plug.

Remove the drain plug to change the oil. When the old oil has drained, install and tighten the plug. Then fill the differential with the correct grade of oil until the level reaches the bottom of the fill/level hole, and install and tighten the plug.

HOW TO INSPECT AND LUBRICATE DRIVESHAFT U-JOINTS

Inspect the driveshaft U-joints for signs of wear, damage, or leakage every time you change the oil. If you have a truck that you drive off-road, you should clean and inspect the joints after every trip.

If you frequently drive in deep water or mud, it's essential that you lubricate the driveshaft slip joints (if your vehicle has them) after every trip or at least once a week during prolonged severe use.

It takes only a couple of minutes to inspect the U-joints and lube the slip joints, and you don't need much:

- A jack, two jack stands, and wheel chocks.

- A grease gun.

- Eye protection.

Raise and support the rear end, making sure it's safely supported and not likely to fall. Then, put the transmission in Neutral and release the parking brake so you can turn the driveshaft, and you're ready to begin.

Check all joints the same way. Two-piece driveshafts will usually have three U-joints and possibly a slip joint. And don't forget the U-joints and CV joints for transfer cases and for axle half-shafts on independent suspension. If you feel any play, replace worn joints as soon as possible.

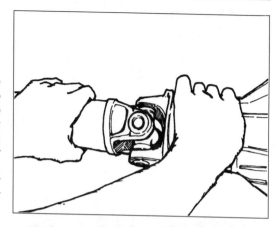

Grasp the driveshaft in one hand and the rear-end yoke in the other. *Turn them back and forth against one another to feel for looseness in the joint. Don't confuse normal gear lash in the differential for play in the U-joint.*

Lubricate the slip joints. *Clean the grease fitting, and push the end of the grease gun nozzle onto it. Pump the gun slowly until the dust seal just starts to bulge. Then, remove the nozzle, and wipe excess grease off of the fitting and the dust seal.*

Lube, Oil, & Chassis Service

HOW TO SERVICE WHEEL BEARINGS

There is a wide variety of wheel hub types and designs in use. Those with unsealed bearings require periodic service. Others, with sealed bearings, are lubricated at the factory and require no further service under normal use.

The illustrations that follow will help you determine which, if any, of your vehicle's wheel bearings require service. Also, check the maintenance schedule in your Owner's Manual to see if wheel bearing service is called for and at what intervals. If wheel bearing service is *not* mentioned, the vehicle has sealed wheel bearings.

Wheel bearing service intervals recommended by most manufacturers are sufficient for normal use and driving conditions. However, for vehicles operated in deep water or mud, wheel bearings should be serviced as soon as possible afterward. Otherwise, the bearings, hubs, and spindles are likely to be damaged, resulting in expensive repairs.

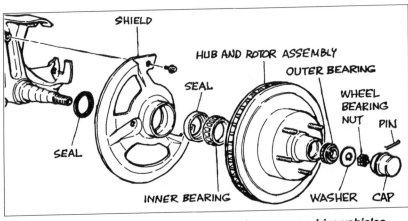

SHIELD

HUB AND ROTOR ASSEMBLY

OUTER BEARING

SEAL

WHEEL BEARING NUT

PIN

SEAL

INNER BEARING

WASHER   CAP

Front wheel bearings on rear-drive vehicles
almost always require periodic lubrication.

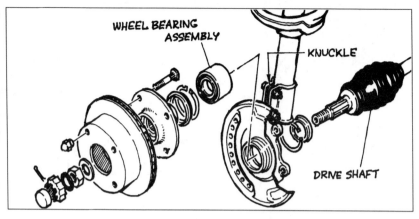

WHEEL BEARING ASSEMBLY

KNUCKLE

DRIVE SHAFT

Front wheel bearings on front-drive vehicles *are usually sealed and require no lubrication service. In most cases adjustment of bearing preload is not required. Work on front-drive hubs requires special tools and skills; it should be left to the pros.*

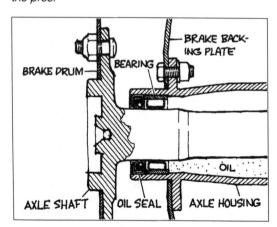

BRAKE BACK-ING PLATE

BRAKE DRUM

BEARING

Rear wheel bearings on rear-drive vehicles *are lubricated by the gear oil in the differential case and do not require service.*

AXLE SHAFT   OIL SEAL   AXLE HOUSING   OIL

To service unsealed bearings, you will need new inner wheel bearing seals, brake cleaner, high-temperature wheel bearing grease, and two new cotter pins to lock the axle nuts in place. You will also need a jack, two jackstands, and wheel chocks, plus an assortment of wrenches and a pair of pliers.

Lube, Oil, & Chassis Service

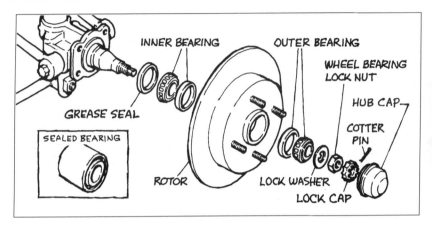

INNER BEARING   OUTER BEARING

WHEEL BEARING
LOCK NUT

HUB CAP

GREASE SEAL

COTTER
PIN

SEALED BEARING

ROTOR   LOCK WASHER

LOCK CAP

Rear wheel bearings on front-drive vehicles
*may or may not require service, depending on
whether or not they are sealed.*

Raise the end of the vehicle you will be
working on, making sure it's safely supported
and not likely to fall. Remove the wheels, and
you're ready to service your wheel bearings.

When you're taking a hub apart be alert to
such things as cotter pins. A very few rear
hubs require high tightening torque on the
axle nuts instead of light bearing preload.
These are easy to recognize because they do
not have cotter pins and castellated (slotted)
nuts. They require a great deal of force to
loosen and tighten the rear axle nuts. Check
with a dealer to make sure you know what
that torque is before servicing this type of hub.

This rear hub does not use cotter pins and castellated nuts. On this particular hub, the plain nut is installed with up to 145 ft-lb of torque. This much force would ruin a hub requiring light bearing preload.

On disc-brake vehicles, remove the calipers. Suspend them out of the way with a coat hanger or cord. Don't let the calipers hang by their hoses, or they could be damaged.

Remove the hub. The drum or rotor will come off with the hub. First remove the grease cap and the cotter pin. Then, unscrew the axle nut, and pull on the rotor or drum to remove the hub from the axle.

**Remove the inner seal
and the bearings from
the hub.** *Rest the hub on
its nose, and pry out the
seal. Be careful not to
damage the seal seat. Lift
out the inner bearing.*

**Clean and inspect the
hub and bearings.** *Clean
old grease from the hub,
the bearing rollers, and
the races. Inspect all
surfaces of the rollers and
the races for chips,
scratches, or other
damage. Check to make
sure the bearings turn
smoothly. If they don't,
replace them.*

**Roll the bearings in your
hand to pack fresh
grease around the
rollers.** *Pack additional
grease in around the
roller ends.*

Set the inner bearing into its race, and turn it several times to seat it. Line up the new seal with the bore in the hub, and carefully tap it into place. You can use a piece of wood to spread the force evenly if the seal is hard to seat. Then, spread a thin film of bearing grease on the lip of the seal.

Install the rotor with the outer bearing in place. Set the bearing into the hub, and the washer on top. Line up the key in the washer with the keyway in the spindle, and hold the bearing in place with your thumbs as you lift the rotor onto the spindle.

Install the spindle nut and adjust bearing preload. Tighten the nut to about 20 ft-lb while turning the rotor or drum several times in each direction to seat the bearing. Then, back off the nut about 60 degrees—that's one flat of the nut.

Install a new cotter pin, and bend the ends of the pin around the spindle. Also, install any nut keepers or locks that you had to remove earlier.

Pack the wheel bearing cap with fresh grease, and install it. Be sure to clean out the old grease first. Tap the rim of the cap gently with a soft mallet in a circular motion until the cap is completely seated.

Finish up the first side by installing the caliper and the wheel. Then, service the opposite wheel in the same way to complete the job.

Finally, road test the vehicle to make sure the brakes are working safely and the hubs are correctly assembled and adjusted. Test the brake pedal for resistance before you begin to drive.

Section 6:

Four-Wheel Drive

SPECIAL 4WD SERVICE REQUIREMENTS

Four-wheel-drive (4WD) vehicles have important special service requirements, even when they are not used off-road. These requirements become even more important as off-road use increases.

An example of a special 4WD service requirement is the constant velocity (CV) joints that connect the transfer case to the front driveshaft. Vehicles with independent front suspension also have CV joints that connect the front axles to the wheels. (CV joints are also called double-Cardan joints because they are actually two U-joints in a single unit.) Most CV joints have flush-mounted grease fittings that require a special adapter for your grease gun.

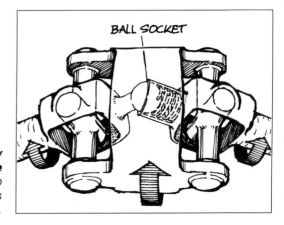

CV joints are actually two U-joints in a single unit. This permits them to operate at extreme angles without binding.

Believe it or not, many four-wheelers don't even know these fittings exist and that the CV joints must be greased frequently. As a result, a great many expensive CV joints are needlessly ruined.

Also, check the differential oil levels after heavy off-road use or fording deep water. Look closely for water in the oil. This can result from leakage around a differential cover seal, but it is more likely that water is entering a differential through worn or damaged axle or pinion shaft seals.

Unique service points on a typical 4WD vehicle. Yours may be different—but not much. Fluid level checks and inspections should be part of your 4WD service routine both at the intervals suggested by the manufacturer as well as immediately after each extended or hard off-road trip.

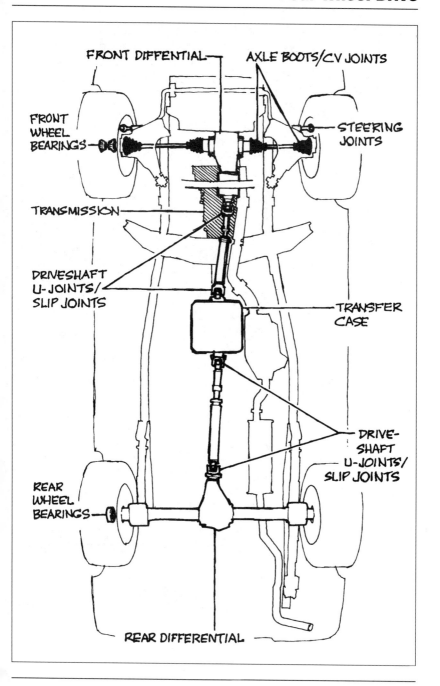

FRONT DIFFENTIAL

AXLE BOOTS/CV JOINTS

FRONT WHEEL BEARINGS

STEERING JOINTS

TRANSMISSION

DRIVESHAFT U-JOINTS/ SLIP JOINTS

TRANSFER CASE

DRIVE-SHAFT U-JOINTS/ SLIP JOINTS

REAR WHEEL BEARINGS

REAR DIFFERENTIAL

HOW TO CHECK AND CHANGE FRONT AND REAR DIFFERENTIAL OIL

Both front and rear axle differentials on 4WD vehicles are filled with heavy oil to lubricate the gears and bearings. Your Owner's Manual specifies the viscosity, type, and how much oil your differentials require.

Check the oil level in the differentials at least once a year or every 15,000 miles. Check them more often if there is any leakage other than slight seepage around the seals.

The oil level should be within 1/4 inch of the bottom of the fill/level hole. Remove the differential fill/level plug and check the level with your finger. If you can't feel the oil, add the correct weight oil until it's up to the bottom of the hole. Then install and tighten the plug. Check both differentials in the same way.

Remove the drain plug to change the oil. When the old oil has drained, install and tighten the plug. Then fill the differential with the correct grade of oil, through the filler hole, until the level reaches the bottom of the hole. Install and tighten the plug. Change the oil in both differentials in the same way.

HOW TO CHECK AND CHANGE TRANSFER CASE OIL

Depending on the design and the manufacturer, transfer case lubricants can be either ATF (automatic transmission fluid), standard multigrade engine oil, or heavy-duty gear oil. For this reason, it's essential that you check your Owner's Manual to determine which type and how much oil your transfer case requires.

Check the transfer case oil level at least once a year or every 15,000 miles. Check it more often if there is any leakage other than slight seepage around the seals.

The oil level should be within 1/4 inch of the bottom of the fill/level hole. Remove the plug and check the level with your finger. If you can't feel the oil, add the correct weight oil until it's up to the bottom of the hole. Then install and tighten the plug.

Remove the drain plug to change the oil. When the old oil has drained, install and tighten the plug. Then fill the transfer case with the correct grade of oil until the level reaches the bottom of the fill/level hole. Install and tighten the plug.

Check the transfer case level immediately following heavy off-road use and after operation in deep water.

Look carefully for the presence of water in the oil. This can result from leakage around a cover seal, but it is more likely that water is entering the transfer case through the shaft seals. If the amount of water is slight and the transfer case was submerged, the seals are probably okay. But, if there is more than just a few drops of water in the oil, the seals are probably worn or damaged and should be replaced.

If you are a moderately experienced do-it-yourselfer you can replace the seals yourself. But you must have a shop manual for your specific vehicle before attempting this work.

HOW TO INSPECT AND LUBRICATE FRONT DRIVESHAFT AND AXLE U-JOINTS AND CV JOINTS

Inspect and lube the driveshaft and axle U-joints and CV joints at each oil change or after an extended or hard off-road drive.

Flush-mounted lube fittings, used in CV joints, require a special adapter for your grease gun. Conventional U-joints may have either flush-mounted fittings or conventional Zerc fittings.

Inspect CV and U-joints for play by grasping the shaft on one side of the joint and the yoke on the other side and turning the shaft back and forth. You shouldn't be able to feel or hear any play in the joint itself.

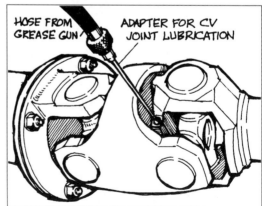

HOSE FROM GREASE GUN

ADAPTER FOR CV JOINT LUBRICATION

Lube CV and U-joints with water-resistant grease. First clean the fitting, push the grease gun tip into the fitting, and pump the grease gun slowly until you see the dust seal start to bulge. Wipe excess grease from the fitting so it won't attract dirt.

A NOTE ON FRONT-WHEEL BEARING SERVICE FOR 4WD

Front wheel bearing service is an essential part of a good 4WD maintenance program. Nevertheless, 4WD front hubs are necessarily quite complex. In addition, there are perhaps a dozen distinct designs in use today, each with its own service procedures and requirements.

The complexity of this task is beyond the scope of this book. If you are a skilled automotive DIYer and want to service your own front hubs, we strongly suggest that you use a shop manual for your specific vehicle. To attempt to work on the hubs without accurate detailed instructions and exploded views is inviting disaster.

Section 7:
Drive Belts

HOW TO INSPECT AND ADJUST DRIVE BELTS

Drive belts are expendable items. Make it a practice to replace them on a regular schedule. An unexpected belt break always puts an unwanted stop in your life!

Check belt condition and tension at least once a month. It takes just a few seconds to spot fraying, cracking, glazing, or burning of the belt contact surfaces—any one of which is reason to replace a belt—right now!

Check the contact surface for cracks and glazing—not just the top of the belt. Cracks are a sign of old age—and a belt that is about to fail. Glazing is caused by slippage. Once it begins, it just gets worse.

Check belt tension. Press in firmly on the belt. You should be able to move the belt in about 1/4 inch midway between the pulleys. If the slack is greater, tighten the belt.

If you find one defective belt, we recommend that you replace them all. Belts all last about the same length of time, and some of the parts you'll have to remove or push out of the way will have to be dealt with whether you're replacing one belt or three.

Also, it's more economical to buy your belts from your favorite auto parts store, rather than from a service station on a Sunday afternoon when you are miles from home.

HOW TO REPLACE DRIVE BELTS

Make sure you buy the correct belts for your vehicle (see page 98). When you remove the old belts, compare them to the new ones to be sure they'll fit. It is acceptable for a new belt to be up to an inch shorter than the old one, which has stretched.

Before you begin replacing belts, study the current arrangement to make sure you know which belt goes on which pulley. We recommend you make a diagram or shoot a few Polaroid photos to avoid error.

This is the most common arrangement for tensioning an alternator drive belt. Both the pivot bolt and the adjuster bolt must be loosened before the alternator can be moved. Just push the alternator toward the engine until the belt is slack enough to come off the pulley.

Tighten the new belt on the alternator by pulling the alternator away from the engine. Apply firm, steady pressure with a pry bar as you tighten the adjuster bolt. Then, tighten the pivot bolt.

Check the tension of the new belt. It should deflect about 1/4 inch when it's first installed and adjusted. After a few hundred miles, check and readjust it.

To loosen or tighten this type of idler pulley, first loosen the lock bolt in the center of the pulley two or three turns. You can then loosen the tensioner bolt to provide slack to remove an old belt. Turn the adjuster the opposite way to tighten a belt, then tighten the pulley bolt to lock the adjuster bolt.

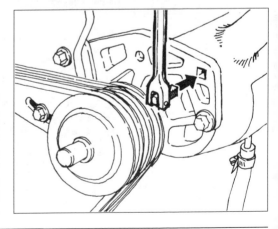

To tension a belt with this type of idler pulley, first loosen the lockbolt then move the idler assembly with a 1/2-inch drive breaker bar or ratchet handle. Hold the idler in position while you tighten the lockbolt.

When installing ribbed belts, *make sure the ribs in the belt line up with the grooves in the pulleys. When this type of belt is off one or more grooves, it will usually rub on the front of the engine or a bracket, creating a loud, persistent squeal.*

WARNING: Never attempt to adjust a belt while the engine is running, or you could injure yourself. If you find a loose belt, shut off the engine, and allow it to cool down before tightening the belts.

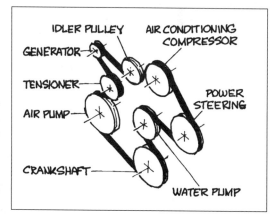

Serpentine belts must be installed to include all driven components and idlers. *If your vehicle has a serpentine belt, check your Owner's Manual for the correct routing.*

PRO TIP: Getting the Right Belts for Your Engine

It used to be that a fan belt was a fan belt. Some were wider or narrower than others and no two seemed to be the same length. But still, buying belts was no big deal.

Today, we're faced with the same old considerations of width and length plus several distinct types—smooth Vee belts, notched Vee belts, ribbed belts, and serpentine belts. Here's an overview.

It's not uncommon for a new belt that's specified for a particular application to be either too long or too short. This can happen when vehicle manufacturers make mid-year changes to brackets or components, or an accessory is added by the dealer.

To make certain you get belts of the right length the first time, first check the old belts for numbers. If the numbers aren't visible, measure the old ones, and then compare those measurements with the ones on the new belts.

New belts are sized on the outside circumference and their length is contained in their number code. If length is not clearly marked on the belt or the sleeve, ask the counterman to interpret the number code for you.

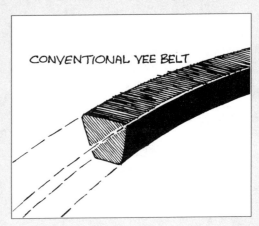

CONVENTIONAL YEE BELT

Conventional Vee belts *are still used on the majority of vehicles.*

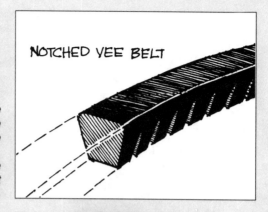

Notched Vee belts are not interchangeable with conventional Vee belts in all cases. Always check the application chart at the store.

Ribbed belts usually drive several components and require low tension because of their large contact area.

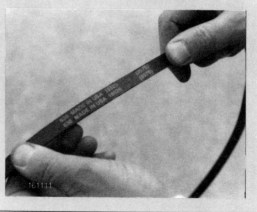

Check the old belts for numbers. Different belt manufacturers use different numbering schemes, but they are all cross referenced in the chart at your auto parts store. Ask for help to get the correct replacement.

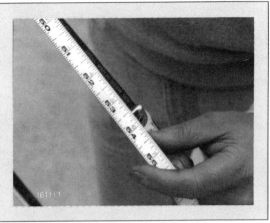

Measure the old belts *to make sure the new ones are the correct length. Mark a spot on the old belt and then measure it with a tape.*

PRO TIP: A Free On-the-Road Emergency Belt Kit

If you replace your drive belts before they get so bad that they break, don't throw away the old ones. Instead, clean them, fold them into small loops, put them in the cardboard sleeves the new belts came in (so you'll have the correct numbers handy), seal them in a plastic bag, and put them in the trunk or spare-tire well for on-the-road emergency use. While old belts may no longer be good enough to trust full time, there is probably enough life left in them to get you home when a belt breaks or is thrown off. And you know they'll fit. Just remember to replace them with new ones as soon as you can, and then put the old ones back into the trunk.

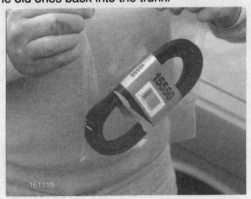

Clean your still-serviceable old belts *and store them in the sleeves the new belts came in. Put the belts in plastic bags and keep them in your vehicle for on-the-road emergency replacement.*

Section 8:
Cooling System

Although we're talking about a major cooling system tune-up, this job is easy, inexpensive, and has an instant payoff as you watch all of the crud being flushed out of your cooling system. To do a major cooling system tune-up you must:

■ Check coolant condition and level.

■ Inspect all hoses and replace bad ones.

■ Inspect the belts and replace bad ones. See Section 7.

■ Inspect "freeze" plugs in the engine.

■ Test the radiator cap and replace it if it won't hold pressure.

- Inspect the fan and fan clutch and replace them if they're worn or damaged.

- Clean the radiator fins.

- Flush and refill the system with fresh antifreeze and water.

WARNING: Make sure the engine is completely cool before working on the cooling system. Coolant at normal engine operating temperatures is under pressure and is hot enough to cause severe burns.

When the gauge registers cold and the radiator is cool to the touch, cover the filler cap with a rag folded into several thicknesses and loosen the cap a quarter turn to relieve the pressure in the system before removing the cap.

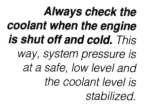

HOW TO CHECK COOLANT LEVEL AND CONDITION

Check engine coolant level in the *radiator* at least once a month. Don't just check the level in the coolant recovery tank; a buildup of deposits on the walls of the tank can make it look like it's full.

Always check the coolant when the engine is shut off and cold. This way, system pressure is at a safe, low level and the coolant level is stabilized.

The coolant's appearance can warn you about cooling system problems. Good coolant is a clear emerald green when it's new, but it will become murky as its anti-corrosive properties decline with use. When it gets murky, change it. It's a good idea to change coolant at least every 2 years or 30,000 miles.

Check for the following conditions:

- **Reddish or milky swirls** in the coolant indicate cooling system rust and corrosion.

- **Black swirls** in the coolant, a milky green color, or oil floating on the surface could be the result of oil leaking past a damaged head gasket.

■ **Milky pink coolant** (in vehicles with automatic transmissions) may indicate a leak in the transmission cooler. Check the transmission fluid for the same condition. If it's also milky pink, have the radiator repaired and the transmission serviced (see also page 68).

If you're constantly adding water, but can't find an external leak, have the cooling system pressure tested by a competent mechanic to find it. (See page 106 for details.)

To top up the coolant, mix equal parts of antifreeze and water. Using a funnel, pour the coolant mixture in through the filler opening until the level is at the base of the opening.

HOW TO INSPECT RADIATOR AND HEATER HOSES

Radiator and heater hoses are expendable items and aren't meant to last forever. If you inspect them regularly you can spot trouble and replace a bad hose before it bursts and strands you on the road.

The hoses should be smooth and free of cracks and damage. Check for internal damage by squeezing the hoses. A mushy feel indicates internal damage. Look for swelling—another sure sign of a hose that's no good.

Many engines are equipped with a thermostat bypass hose that allows the pump to circulate coolant even when the thermostat is closed. This hose should be inspected—and changed—with the other hoses.

Inspect the heater hoses. Like the radiator hoses, these should be smooth and free of cracks, damage, and swelling.

PRESSURE TESTING THE RADIATOR CAP AND COOLING SYSTEM

The cooling system must maintain good pressure to cool properly. Water boils at 212°F in an uncovered container. In a sealed cooling system, the boiling point is raised to 240° to 250°F. A leaking cap or radiator hose will lose coolant, and will also lower the boiling point of the system. When this happens, you lose your "safety margin" for hot weather driving and driving under sustained loads.

We recommend that you pressure test your system only when you have either (1) an overheating problem or (2) unexplained coolant loss—where you cannot locate an obvious leak.

Pressure testing the radiator cap and the cooling system is something we recommend you leave to your local full-service gas station or radiator specialty shop. As infrequently as you need to do this test, it's not worth buying a tester. Once the leak has been located, you'll be able to fix it—unless it's in the radiator or an engine block freeze plug.

Correcting a leaking radiator is a job for a radiator shop. More experienced DIYer's can save the labor charge of removal and replacement. But the repair itself requires special equipment and skills.

Have your radiator cap and cooling system pressure tested by a competent professional with the proper test equipment.

A leaking freeze plug is much more difficult to correct. The old plug must be removed from the block and a new plug installed. Occasionally it's possible to do this with the engine in the vehicle. However, this should be regarded as a temporary repair. When one freeze plug begins to leak others may soon follow.

The best way to replace freeze plugs in most engines is with the engine out of the vehicle. We do *not* recommend engine removal and replacement for the average DIYer.

An expanding rubber plug works well for a temporary fix of a leaking freeze plug when you can remove the old plug with the engine in place.

Lube, Oil, & Chassis Service

HOW TO REPLACE THE THERMOSTAT

Your engine's thermostat is a control valve that regulates operating temperature in a range that's best for your engine. It does this by controlling the flow of coolant between the engine and the radiator. When the engine is cold, the thermostat holds the coolant in the engine where it heats up rapidly to operating temperature. When the engine is warmed up, the thermostat opens to allow coolant to flow through the radiator.

The thermostat is almost always located at the base of the top radiator hose. In this typical example, just two bolts hold the thermostat cover in place. It's not absolutely necessary to disconnect the radiator hose, although the job is easier if you do.

If the thermostat fails in the closed position, the engine will overheat. If the thermostat fails in the open position, the engine won't warm up properly. In either case, the thermostat must be replaced.

This is an easy job, but you will have to drain and refill the cooling system, and, on some vehicles, do a bit of disassembly. Make sure you have the replacement thermostat and gasket on hand before you start. A 180-degree or 190-degree thermostat is recommended by most manufacturers.

This is a good time to do a full cooling system service, including a flush (see page 115).

The engine shown in this procedure is a Chevy V8. It's not significantly different from an equivalent Ford or Chrysler engine and is representative of at least three fourths of the cars and trucks on the road today.

Before starting this job, *allow the engine to cool completely.* Even when warm, the coolant is under considerable pressure and could cause injury. When the engine is cool, release cooling system pressure by loosening the radiator cap one-quarter turn. Then, when pressure is relieved, remove the cap and drain the radiator. If the coolant is in good condition and no more than six months old, drain it into a clean container so you can reuse it. Otherwise, refill the system as described on page 118.

Remove the upper radiator hose. *Loosen the clamps and disconnect the hose from the thermostat cover. Twist the hose a quarter-turn to break it loose and pull it off the spigot.*

Lube, Oil, & Chassis Service

Remove the thermostat cover and thermostat. Place rags around the cover to catch leaking coolant. Remove the bolts. Gently tap the cover with a mallet to break it loose. Make a mental note of the orientation of the thermostat. In most cases, the spring will be on the bottom.

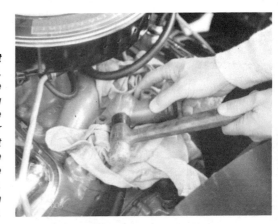

Scrape any gasket material from the sealing surfaces with a putty knife or similar tool. Take care not to gouge the metal. If an O-ring seal is used, clean the O-ring groove on the engine and on the housing. Remove all the old gasket material from the thermostat housing or it can clog radiator passages.

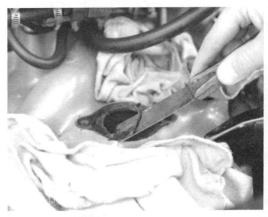

Put a very thin coat of sealer on both sides of the gasket. Don't "gob" it on or it may wind up in the thermostat and jam it either open or closed.

Install the new thermostat and new gasket or O-ring. *Any marks such as TOP or UP should face up. Otherwise, the spring side of the thermostat should face down and the gasket fits on top of it.*

Install the thermostat cover. *Tighten the bolts by hand to seat the cover, then torque them to about 15 ft-lb. Then, connect the hose, and fill the system.*

Before driving the vehicle, start the engine, and check for leaks. Pay particular attention to the thermostat cover and the hose connections. Correct any leaks before driving the vehicle.

Lube, Oil, & Chassis Service

HOW TO REPLACE RADIATOR AND HEATER HOSES

We think it's a good idea to replace all radiator hoses and heater hoses at the same time. When you spot swelling, cracking, and deterioration in one, the others can't be far behind. Besides, when you replace a complete set, you can be confident of long-term reliability. We also think it's a good idea to flush the cooling system and fill it with fresh antifreeze and water (see page 118).

Compare new hoses to the old ones before removing them to make sure they are correct. Also note how the old hose is installed so you can install the new one the same way. When buying heater hoses, measure the outside diameter of *both* old hoses to be sure the new ones are the correct sizes. One hose is usually larger than the other.

Begin the job by draining the system.

WARNING: There is a risk of skinning your knuckles when the old hoses suddenly come off their fittings. A simple way to avoid injuring your hands is to wear heavy work gloves when pulling and twisting off the hoses.

Before starting this job, *allow the radiator and engine to cool completely*. Even when just warm, the coolant is under considerable pressure and could cause injury. When the radiator is cool to the touch, cover the filler cap with a rag folded into several thicknesses, and loosen the cap one-quarter turn to relieve the pressure in the system. Then remove the cap and drain the system.

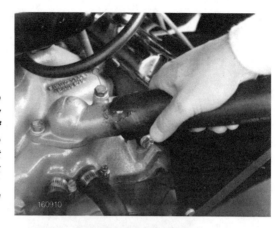

Remove the hose clamps, and carefully slice through the end of the old hose. *Twist the old hose about one-quarter turn to break it loose from the spigot. Then pull it off using steady pressure.*

Clean the engine and radiator spigots *with a wire brush to remove scale and rust. This will help the new hoses seal leak free.*

Position the clamps about 1/8 inch from the ends of the hose, *and make sure the clamps are snug. Don't tighten them so much that they cut into the hose.*

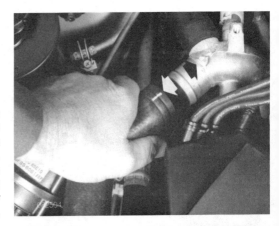

Some long hoses with lots of bends have locater marks on the hose ends and spigots. Just line up the mark on the hose with the mark on the spigot to correctly route the hose.

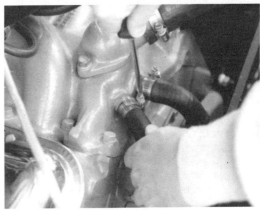

Install new heater hoses (and thermostat bypass hose if so equipped) just like you did with the radiator hoses.

Flush the system (as described on the next page), and refill it with new coolant and water (as described on page 118).

Warm up the engine to normal operating temperature, shut it off, and check all connections for leaks.

HOW TO FLUSH THE COOLING SYSTEM

Flushing the cooling system every year helps ensure maximum cooling efficiency. We recommend you flush the system after pressure testing and repairing a leak, replacing the thermostat, or replacing hoses. Anytime you are draining and replacing coolant, why not flush the system and keep it clean?

In addition to a flushing fitting (see page 117) you'll need a can of cooling system flush/cleaner. If you've changed coolant in the last couple of years, a normal strength cleaner should do the job. If the system hasn't been serviced for longer than you can remember, use a heavy-duty cleaner.

This is an easy job, but allow yourself several hours. The engine must be filled and flushed and allowed to cool a couple of times. In cases of extreme rust and scale buildup, the entire system—engine and radiator—should be power flushed by a radiator shop.

Set the heater controls to the full HOT position.
This will allow the coolant to drain from the heater core.

Lube, Oil, & Chassis Service

Drain the system before flushing it. *If you can't locate a drain plug on the radiator, disconnect the bottom radiator hose to allow both the radiator and engine to drain. Then, close the drain or reconnect the hose.*

Use coolant system flush to loosen scale and rust from the system. *Pour the cleaner directly into the radiator, then fill the system with fresh water. Follow the manufacturer's instructions for the amount of time the engine must run with the cleaner in the system.*

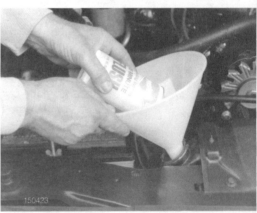

Allow the engine to cool down before connecting the flushing fitting *to a garden hose. Flush the cooling system with the engine running at 1,500-2,000 rpm until the water running out of the radiator opening is clear.*

PRO TIP: How to Install a Flushing Fitting

You have to wonder why cars and trucks aren't equipped with this inexpensive device when new. Flushing fittings are sold in most auto parts stores, and installation takes about 5 minutes and requires only a craft knife and a screwdriver.

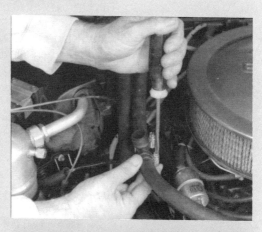

First, cut the return (in-flow) hose from the engine to the heater with a sharp craft knife. Then, rejoin the hose with the flushing fitting and two hose clamps. (The in-flow hose is connected to the engine farther away from the water pump than the out-flow hose.)

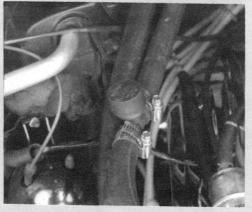

Connect a garden hose to the flushing fitting, and you're ready to flush the system. When flushing is completed, disconnect the garden hose, and seal the fitting with the cap that is supplied with it.

HOW TO REFILL THE COOLING SYSTEM

The best mixture for your cooling system is 50-percent antifreeze and 50-percent water. Too little antifreeze results in loss of protection against corrosion and freezing, and too much antifreeze causes the engine to run hotter than normal.

The easiest way to get a 50/50 mix is first determine how much coolant your system holds. Check your Owner's Manual, or ask the counterperson when you buy your antifreeze. (Most stores have this information to help you buy the correct amount of antifreeze you need.) Next, divide the cooling system capacity by 2. For example, if your system holds 16 quarts, half of that is 8 quarts, or 2 gallons. (For those vehicles with the capacity given in liters, 1 liter is just slightly more than 1 quart. For example 16 quarts is about 15 liters.)

Once the system is filled, install and tighten the filler cap (and install the air relief bolt if your system has one). Run the engine at 1,500-2,000 rpm for about a minute, and check for leaks from the radiator drain valve and the hoses. Don't tighten anything while the engine is running; you could be injured by the fan or drive belts. Shut the engine off and let it cool completely before correcting leaks.

Finally, with the engine completely cool, check and correct the coolant level. Carefully open the filler cap to the first notch to vent all system pressure. Then, remove the cap and add water to bring the level up to the bottom of the filler opening and install the cap.

Pour the correct amount of antifreeze (half of the system capacity) into the radiator. *Then, fill the system with fresh water until it comes up to the base of the filler neck in the radiator, and install the radiator cap.*

Vent the system, if you can. *Some systems have an air relief bolt or valve located near the highest point in the cooling system. This permits trapped air to escape from the system as it is filled and ensures that the system will be completely filled.*

Warm up the engine to circulate coolant through the entire system. *Then, turn off the engine, allow it to cool completely, and check and correct the level in the radiator with more water.*

QUICK CHECK TABLE: Freeze protection vs. Antifreeze Concentration

This table shows how more antifreeze can prevent freezing in extremely cold weather. Our 50/50 recommendation should be adequate for most situations.

Freezing temperature °F (°C)	Safe operating temperature °F (°C)	Antifreeze concentration
3 (-16)	12 (-11)	30%
-4 (-20)	5 (-15)	35%
-13 (-25)	-4 (-20)	40%
-22 (-30)	-13 (-25)	45%
-33 (-36)	-24 (-31)	50%
-44 (-42)	-35 (-37)	55%
-58 (-50)	-49 (-45)	60%

Section 9:

Brake System

**HOW TO CHECK
AND
REPLENISH
BRAKE FLUID**

HOW TO CHECK AND REPLENISH BRAKE FLUID

While correct brake fluid level is important, the *condition* of the fluid is equally important. The appearance of the fluid can tell you when it should be changed so you can avoid potentially dangerous and expensive brake system problems.

Here's what happens: Brake fluid is "hygroscopic," which means that it absorbs water. If it didn't, water that's produced by condensation in the system could collect in the wheel cylinders and calipers and cause corrosion. Also, the heat from the brakes will boil the water and cause a loss of braking power. Eventually, brake fluid absorbs all the water it can hold. If it's not changed at this point—or before—the excess water collects in the wheel cylinders and calipers and begins to damage them.

When it's in good condition, brake fluid is a transparent honey color. If the fluid is murky, it's contaminated by moisture and should be replaced immediately (see page 135). Brake fluid should be changed every 2 years or 30,000 miles under normal driving conditions.

On plastic reservoirs, the fluid level should be between the lines, and never lower than the bottom minimum-level line. If the level is close to but still above the minimum-level line, don't add fluid but do inspect the pads and shoes for wear and the entire system for leaks (see page 125).

On well-type reservoirs, the level should be within 1/2 inch of the upper edge. If the level is lower than 1 inch from the top, inspect the pads and shoes for wear and the system for leaks before adding fluid.

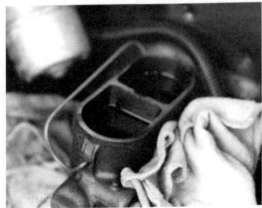

Unless otherwise specified in your Owner's Manual or on the reservoir cover, use only DOT Type 3 brake fluid that has been stored in a sealed container. If you already have fluid but are unsure of its condition, don't use it. We recommend buying fluid in the smallest container possible (unless you're changing all the fluid in the system). Once the can has been opened, brake fluid doesn't keep very well. It goes right to work absorbing moisture from the air!

Do not add other fluids, such as transmission fluid or oil. They will damage the system and lead to brake failure.

Don't splash or drip brake fluid onto painted surfaces or it will cause damage. Wipe up spills immediately and wash the surface with soapy water.

Add fluid slowly to prevent aeration and overfilling. Reinstall the reservoir cap snugly so there is no danger of leakage or of air getting into the system.

PRO TIP: What Brake Fluid Level Can Tell You About Brake Wear

When the level in the brake fluid reservoir drops a little, it's okay—as long as there aren't any leaks in the brake system. That falling level is telling you that you should inspect the pads and shoes for wear.

As brake pads and shoes wear down, the pistons in the calipers and wheel cylinders must move farther to push the pads and shoes into contact with the discs and drums. To do this, the pistons require more brake fluid. This is supplied by the reservoir on the master cylinder. So, as the level in the reservoir drops, it's telling you that the pads and shoes are wearing down.

As long as the level is above the minimum safe-level mark, there's no need to add fluid. As the fluid level nears the minimum-level mark, inspect the pads and shoes for wear (see page 125). And, if the level falls suddenly, inspect the brake system for leaks.

When the brake fluid is near the minimum safe-level line, it's telling you to inspect the brake pads and shoes for wear. Then it's okay to add brake fluid.

HOW TO INSPECT DISC BRAKES

The majority of cars and light trucks on the road today are equipped with front disc brakes. Some cars have disc brakes on all four wheels. Although there are many specific models of disc brakes, inspection is similar for all.

While the differences between brake models have little effect on inspection, even minor work such as pad replacement requires special instructions and information to ensure safe completion. If the brake inspection described here indicates that work is needed, either have it done by a competent brake specialist or, if you will be doing it yourself, use the appropriate factory service manual.

You should inspect your brakes every 10,000-15,000 miles of normal service, or sooner if you do a lot of hard braking or haul or tow heavy loads. Also inspect the brakes immediately if the fluid level in the reservoir is near its bottom safe limit (see page 124), or if you hear a high-pitched squeal—from the brake wear indicators—or any scraping or grinding noises when you apply the brakes.

Raise and support the front of the vehicle and remove the wheels, making sure the vehicle is safely supported and not likely to fall. Then, locate the brake pad inspection "window" in the caliper. On some models you will have to remove a cover from the window.

Next, place a few layers of old newspaper under the brakes, put on your dust mask or respirator, and use brake cleaner to remove brake dust and dirt from both the inside and outside of the caliper. Now you're ready to inspect the brakes.

Lube, Oil, & Chassis Service

PRO TIP: Beware of Brake Dust

Brake dust residue may contain asbestos and is hazardous if inhaled or consumed. We urge you to follow just a few simple rules when working on brakes:

1. Always wear a respirator or painter's mask when you are working on brakes.

2. Don't blow dust away with compressed air. Use damp rags to remove the dust.

3. When all the dust has been removed, seal the rags in a plastic bag and dispose of them.

4. At the completion of brake work, immediately wash your hands thoroughly. Then, take a shower and launder your work clothes.

To avoid asbestos danger, we recommend you specify "semi-metallic" pads and shoes when you replace brake linings. They cost more, but last longer.

Check pad thickness. If they're worn to a thickness equal to the backing plate, they should be replaced immediately, before you need expensive brake work.

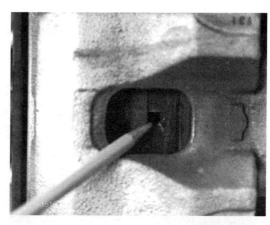

If the pads have wear indicators they should still be visible. If the indicator mark or groove is worn off on just one pad, the entire set is ready for replacement.

Check the rotor. The surface should be smooth, although some minor scoring is likely to occur in time. If the scores are deep enough to snag your fingernail, the rotor should be resurfaced or replaced.

Check the flexible hoses for damage or deterioration. Look for wetness—a sign of brake fluid leaks. Clean the hose and gently bend it at several points to check for cracks or splits, as well as brittleness or sponginess. Your life rides on your brakes, so replace any flexible brake hoses that are less than perfect.

PRO TIP: Why Disc Brakes Squeal and How to Fix Them

One of the most common complaints car owners have is about annoying brake squeal. Annoying or not, there is a time when brake squeal is a good thing—if you know what's causing it and what to do about it.

Most inner brake pads have an audible wear indicator to warn you that your brake pads are just about worn out and should be replaced. When the pad wears down to the point that it should be replaced, the metal wear indicator makes contact with the disc each time the brakes are applied. This creates a harmless high-pitched squeal that warns you that you are about out of brake pad material. If you ignore the warning, you will soon hear a louder squeal as the metal pad backing plate makes contact with the disc. This squeal is not harmless. It's the sound of grooves being cut into your discs, turning them into junk!

When the metal wear indicator makes contact with the disc each time the brakes are applied, it makes a harmless high-pitched squeal to warn that you are about out of brake pad material. Don't ignore the warning, or the metal backing plate behind the brake pad will destroy the disc!

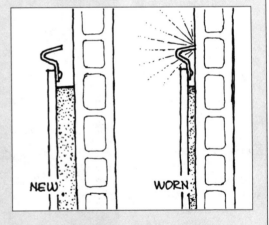

There's another type of brake squeal that's not good—but it's not likely to cause major damage. This is squeal caused by the brake pads vibrating against the discs at high frequency. Often, this occurs right after new brake pads have been installed.

If this type of brake squeal occurs, remove the pads and the anti-squeal shims and clean them. Then, apply a thin coat of high-temperature brake silicone to the back of the pads, where they contact the shims. Also apply silicone to the shims where they contact the caliper and piston. The silicone dampens the vibration and should eliminate the squeal. Use only a light coat of silicone, and be sure to keep it off the friction material of the pads and off the disc. This is not guaranteed to solve every brake squeal problem, but it is effective 70 percent of the time.

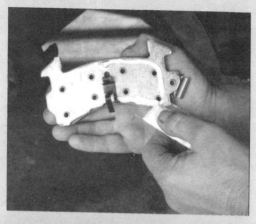

To apply high-temperature brake silicone to pads, begin with a narrow bead around the edge. A modest amount will do the job.

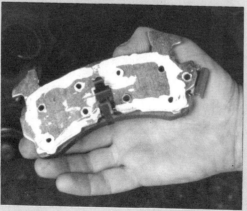

Spread the silicone into a thin film, and allow it to "cure" for several minutes. Then install the pads. Incidentally, brake silicone is often supplied with new replacement pads to help avoid squeal.

HOW TO BLEED THE BRAKE SYSTEM

The brakes must be bled when air has entered the system, either because of excessively low fluid level in the reservoir or a break in the system.

A spongy pedal and poor brake performance are sure signs of air in the system. You might not realize you've lost braking power until you need your brakes in an emergency—when it's too late to do anything about it. So, as soon as you feel any sponginess, check the fluid level and inspect the entire system for leaking fluid—a sign of a break that could allow air to enter the system. Make sure any leaks are fixed before you bleed the system.

Brake systems can be bled either manually or with a pressure bleeder. There are many types of pressure bleeders, so if you are using one, follow the pressure bleeder manufacturer's instructions.

The instructions here are for manual bleeding. You'll need fresh brake fluid, a bleeder valve wrench, a 2-foot length of clean, clear plastic tubing, a clean glass jar, and an assistant.

If air entered through the master cylinder (level too low), begin by bleeding it as shown on the next page. Otherwise, you may skip that step and just bleed air at the four wheels.

To bleed the master cylinder, disconnect the front line, then reconnect but don't tighten it. Depress and hold the pedal to expel air, and tighten the fitting before releasing the pedal. Wait 15 seconds and do it again until all air has been removed from the front chamber. Now do the same for the rear chamber and you're ready to do the wheels.

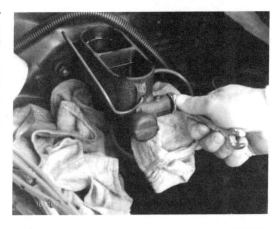

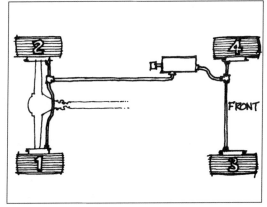

The most common brake bleeding sequence is: Right rear, Left rear, Right front, and Left front.

Follow the simple sequence described below. Start with a full fluid reservoir.

1. Have your assistant sit in the driver's seat, ready to operate the brake pedal.

2. Clean the bleeder valve on the right rear brake and connect the bleeder hose to it. Place the other end of the hose in a clear glass jar with the end of the hose submerged in fresh brake fluid. This prevents air from getting into the system.

3. Using the command "Down," have your assistant press and hold the brake pedal. (Don't press the pedal all the way to the floor; it could damage the master cylinder.)

4. Open the bleeder valve one-half turn to release trapped air, then close it.

5. Using the command "Up," have your assistant release the brake pedal.

6. Have your assistant press and hold the pedal—"Down."

7. Open the bleeder valve one-half turn to release trapped air, then quickly close it.

8. Have your assistant release the brake pedal—"Up."

9. Top up the fluid reservoir. Repeat this step every three full Up/Down sequences.

10. Have your assistant press and hold the pedal—"Down."

11. Open the bleeder valve one-half turn to release trapped air, then close it.

12. Have your assistant release the brake pedal—"Up."

13. Have your assistant press and hold the pedal—"Down."

. . . And so on. Keep up this routine until the fluid running out of the end of the hose is clear and free of bubbles—and free of air. When you're done with the first wheel, move on to the next one in the sequence and repeat the routine at all four wheels.

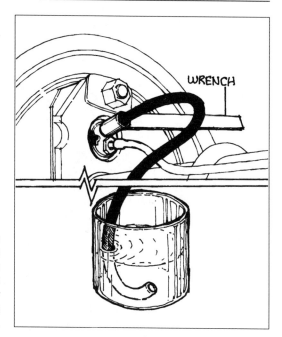

Begin bleeding with the brake farthest from the master cylinder. *Clean the valve and connect the hose, submerge the other end in a glass jar of fresh brake fluid.*

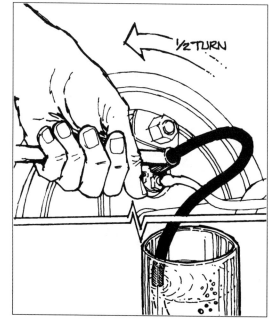

Have an assistant press and hold the brake pedal *while you open the bleeder valve one-half turn to release trapped air. Then close the valve before releasing the pedal. Continue with this sequence—"Down," open the valve, close the valve, "Up," etc. until there is no air in the fluid coming from the hose and the pedal feels firm.*

When the entire system has been correctly bled, the pedal will feel firm when you press and hold it. Top up the master cylinder and install the cap tightly. Then, road test the brakes, beginning at low speed until you are sure they are working correctly. But before you move the vehicle, test the pedal firmness.

__Keep up the level in the master cylinder.__ If it falls too low, air will be drawn into the system and you'll have to start all over. When the system has been correctly bled, the pedal will feel firm. Top up the master cylinder, install the cap tightly, and road test the brakes at low speed until you are sure they're okay.

HOW TO FLUSH THE BRAKE SYSTEM AND REPLACE THE FLUID

The brake system should be flushed and the fluid replaced every 2 years or 30,000 miles under normal driving conditions. This should also be done, without regard to time or mileage, when the fluid is contaminated with moisture and becomes murky (see page 121).

Flushing is like bleeding the system in that the wheel cylinders and calipers are individually flushed. Flushing differs from bleeding in that each bleeder valve is opened 1-1/2 turns and fluid is forced through the wheel cylinder or caliper until the fluid is clear and honey colored. As a result, flushing the system will consume more fluid than bleeding it. So, be sure to keep the reservoir full of fresh brake fluid so you won't draw air into the system. Count on refilling the reservoir several times and using as much as a quart of new brake fluid.

Follow the instructions for bleeding the brake system (see page 130), remembering to open the bleeder valves fully to allow the new fluid to flush the system.

When flushing the system, open bleeder valves 1-1/2 turns. Do not submerge the end of the hose in the old fluid or you won't be able to see when it begins to run clear. Continue to flush each wheel cylinder or caliper until the fluid running out of the hose is clear.

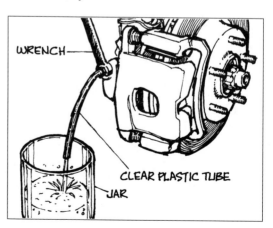

WRENCH

CLEAR PLASTIC TUBE

JAR

Section 10:
Shock Absorbers

HOW SHOCK ABSORBERS WORK

Shock absorbers are a vital part of your vehicle's suspension system. When your wheels hit a bump, the springs compress to absorb energy that would otherwise be transmitted to the body. Once a spring is set in motion, it will continue to oscillate, or bounce, until the absorbed energy is used up. Shock absorbers control the springs' motion by using up the stored energy and provide a smooth, controllable ride.

In time, shocks lose their effectiveness as the piston seals wear. In most cases, the loss in ride control is so gradual you don't notice it in daily driving. For this reason it's important that you test the shock absorbers regularly to determine if they are worn and need replacement.

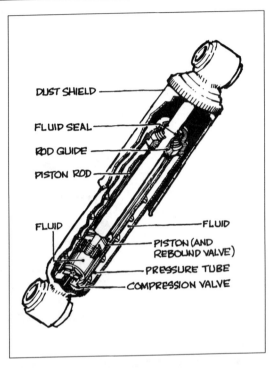

DUST SHIELD

FLUID SEAL

ROD GUIDE

PISTON ROD

FLUID

FLUID

PISTON (AND
REBOUND VALVE)

PRESSURE TUBE

COMPRESSION VALVE

*A shock absorber consists of a piston that
moves up and down in a fluid-filled tube* as the
spring compresses and extends. The fluid resists
the piston's motion to stop the spring from
bouncing.

HOW TO TEST SHOCK ABSORBERS

Test the shocks one at a time by pushing down on one corner of the vehicle and releasing it. It should rock down, rise up just once, and immediately settle to it's normal height. If it rocks down again before settling, the shocks will need replacement soon. If it continues to bob several times, you need new shocks.

Visually inspect the shock absorbers for leakage and damage. If a shock is leaking oil around the shaft, it should be replaced, even if it passed the bounce test.

Check all mounting points for tightness. Twist the shocks to check for play in the bushings. If they are worn, replace them and the shocks. Tighten all shock mounting nuts and bolts. If they are loose they can damage mounting studs and bosses which can require expensive repairs.

HOW TO REPLACE SHOCK ABSORBERS

Always replace shock absorbers in pairs or complete sets. This ensures equal motion damping on both wheels on the same "axle." You'll need some silicone lubricant—like WD-40—and possibly some rust penetrant for stubborn nuts and bolts. You'll also need safety glasses to protect your eyes when you are under the vehicle. It's possible to replace shocks on some vehicles without raising them. However, if you must lift yours you will need a jack, two jack stands, and wheel chocks. Make sure the vehicle is safely supported and not likely to fall.

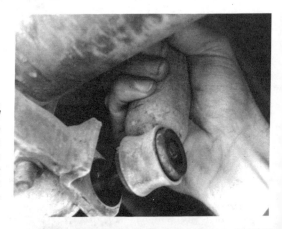

On double-eye shocks, remove the nuts and pull or tap the shock off of the mounts. If it's a gas shock, tap the bottom eye off of its mount first, but be careful—the shock will probably extend quickly and the axle will also drop.

Post-type shock mounts must be prevented from turning when the nut is removed or installed. Use either small Vise Grips or a 3/16-inch (or 5-mm) open-end wrench to hold the post.

Remove all dirt and rust from shock mounts *before installing new shocks. This prevents binding and allows the shocks to work freely.*

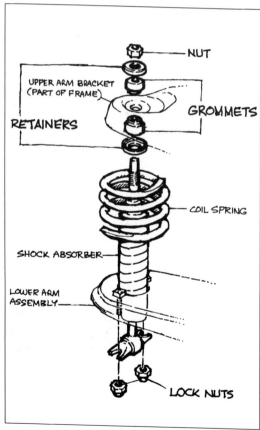

NUT

UPPER ARM BRACKET (PART OF FRAME)

RETAINERS

GROMMETS

COIL SPRING

SHOCK ABSORBER

LOWER ARM ASSEMBLY

LOCK NUTS

Use all the hardware supplied with the new shocks. *The large flat washers and sleeves supplied with some shocks hold the shocks in place without binding, even when fully extended or compressed. Spray grommets with silicone lubricant before installing them. Don't cut the safety wire on new gas shocks until the shocks are installed and all nuts are tightened. If necessary, use a jack to lift the frame or suspension to line up the mounting points.*

141

HOW TO SELECT THE RIGHT SHOCKS

There are replacement shock absorbers built for all types of driving. The trick is finding the one you need. Here's a quick rundown on what type of shocks are available and what they are designed to do.

Standard-duty shocks are like the original equipment on most vehicles. They work okay if most of your driving is on smooth roads and streets and you are not constantly carrying heavy loads or lots of passengers.

Standard-duty shocks provide a soft, smooth ride but can't handle the severe, sharp jolts of poor roads and heavy cargo. Frankly, we never use them for replacements. This is an opportunity to improve handling with heavy-duty shocks or air shocks.

**Standard-duty shocks are usually slim.** A 1-inch diameter valve body is common with this type, and the lower tube is usually no larger than 1-1/4 to 1-1/2 inches in diameter.

Standard—or "OEM"—shocks are the cheapest replacement, but also wear out faster than heavy-duty types.

Heavy-duty shocks have more damping action than standard shocks, and most are gas-charged. This permits them to handle severe bumps and holes on poor roads and to provide a firmer ride and more control with heavy loads. The stable feel of heavy-duty shocks is accompanied by a firm ride that some find objectionable.

Better-quality heavy-duty shocks have 1-3/8 to 1-1/2-inch valve bodies and are bigger than standard shocks with lower legs 1-3/4 to 2 inches in diameter. Budget heavy-duty shocks have 1-inch valve bodies and rely on special valving to slow down the oil and increase damping. Although this type is cheaper than the large heavy-duty types, they will not last as long, particularly under continued severe use. We like large-diameter gas-filled heavy duty shocks for most applications.

Heavy-duty shocks are usually larger in diameter than standard shocks, and are usually gas filled. They have larger 1-3/8 to 1-1/2-inch diameter valve bodies.

Do be aware that gas-filled shocks can raise the ride height of your vehicle. One inch is typical.

Air shocks are variable overload shocks that can be quickly "tuned" to the size of the load. Used on the rear only, air shocks do the same job as spring-assisted overload shocks—but only when extra support is needed.

For heavy loads, you inflate air shocks to a pressure suggested by the manufacturer, depending on the weight of the load. Then, when you're ready to resume normal light-duty use, you reduce the air pressure, usually to about 20 psi, and you have a smooth, comfortable ride again.

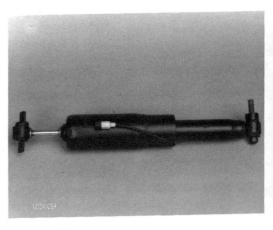

Air shocks are for vehicles which occasionally haul heavy loads. Used on the rear, air shocks do the same job as overload shocks—but only when needed.

What's the downside to air shocks? Besides costing more, they do add complexity and vulnerability. The air fill lines and Schrader valves can be damaged. However, if you sometimes carry heavy loads, we recommend them highly. Not only do they restore ride height, they provide better vehicle stability.

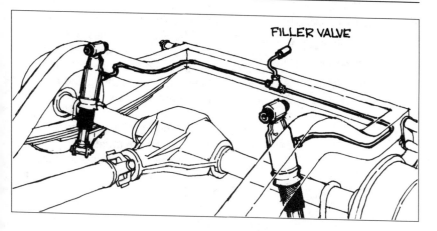

FILLER VALVE

Air pressure is increased or decreased through a single valve. *This ensures equal pressure in both shocks. The valve should be located outside of the cargo area. Lines must be routed away from exhaust pipes and suspension.*

SHOCK ABSORBER MOUNTING BASICS

There are about a half-dozen methods for mounting shock absorbers. They're shown and described here so you will have some idea of what you'll encounter in replacing shocks, and will be able to recognize the mounts you need on new shocks.

No matter what type of mounting points are used, all shock absorbers must be mounted securely without any play. Mounts that are damaged, either through rust or wear, should be repaired or replaced.

Spray all soft bushings with silicone lubricant such as WD-40 before installing them. Then, spray them again after installation to protect them and help keep them supple.

Replace damaged removable studs and bolts. Non-removable mounting studs can often be repaired with new sleeves. Check with your auto parts store for replacement sleeves.

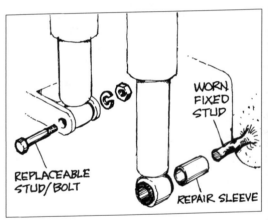

REPLACEABLE STUD/BOLT

WORN FIXED STUD

REPAIR SLEEVE

Worn mounting holes in the frame or suspension should be repaired with washers welded over the old holes. Make sure the hole in the washer is the same size as the shock mounting bolt.

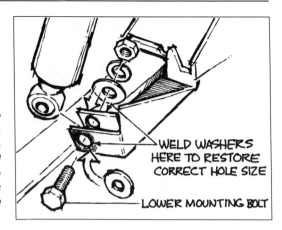

WELD WASHERS HERE TO RESTORE CORRECT HOLE SIZE

LOWER MOUNTING BOLT

A coned wheel nut will tighten up a worn lower shock mounting hole if it's only slightly worn. Make sure the shock mounting bolt is the correct size for the coned nut.

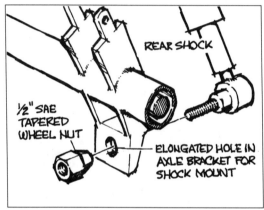

REAR SHOCK

½" SAE TAPERED WHEEL NUT

ELONGATED HOLE IN AXLE BRACKET FOR SHOCK MOUNT

Eye with rubber bushing. This mount can be used on either the top or bottom or on both ends.

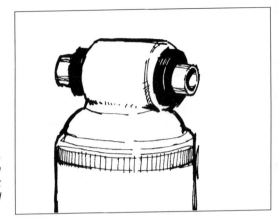

Eye with metal insert.
This mount is often
used where the shock
fits between two fixed
plates or panels.

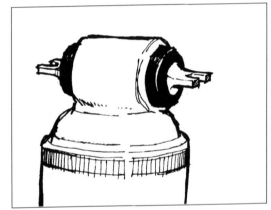

**Eye with two-bolt
crossbar.** This type
mount comes with the
crossbar installed, usually
in a rubber bushing.

**Eye with right-angle
stud.** The shock comes
with the stud installed,
either rigid or in a rubber
bushing.

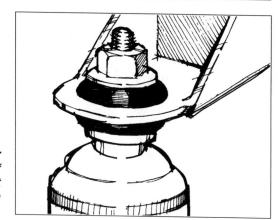

Stud mount with rubber bushings. *This is one of the most common mount types and can be used on one or both ends.*

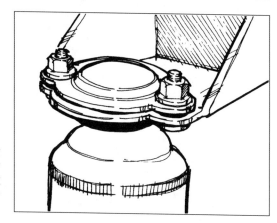

Bolted plate. *This mount is common where the shock is mounted in sheet metal in unit-construction vehicles.*

A NOTE ON SHOCK ABSORBER CARTRIDGE REPLACEMENT IN STRUT SUSPENSION

Like conventional shock absorbers, the cartridges in McPherson-strut suspension must be occasionally replaced. This is not an easy job. Before a strut can be removed from the car, the spring must be compressed. This requires a special tool. Then, the car and the suspension must be supported independently of one another. In some cases, removal requires expensive special tools. The strut must be disassembled to replace the cartridge. The compressed spring makes this step potentially very dangerous. If the compressor were to slip off of a spring, you could be seriously injured. For these reasons, we strongly recommend that you have McPherson strut shock cartridges replaced by a competent pro.

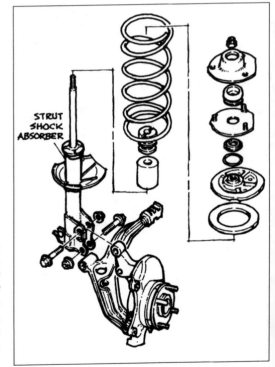

The complexity of a suspension strut is obvious in this typical example. A great deal of suspension disassembly is required to get a strut to this stage, where it can be disassembled and the shock cartridge replaced.

STRUT SHOCK ABSORBER

Section 11:

Exhaust System

HOW TO INSPECT THE EXHAUST SYSTEM

The two worst enemies of the exhaust system are heat and moisture. Expansion and contraction from heating and cooling stresses the system gaskets and joints. Moisture—the main by-product of combustion—condenses on the inside walls of the pipes and mufflers and collects at the lowest points in the system, causing rust and corrosion.

Inspect the entire exhaust system every six months, looking for corrosion and damage that could allow dangerous fumes to enter the passenger compartment. The inspection is easy to do on a service hoist, and you can also do it by raising and supporting one end of the vehicle at a time, and sliding underneath on your back.

Exhaust systems are notorious for developing a fine layer of rust that comes off even when you lightly touch it, so wear good eye protection when you make your inspection.

Make sure the exhaust system is completely cool before inspecting it. Otherwise, you could be burned. Pay particular attention to catalytic converters which get so hot that they can still burn you when the rest of the system has cooled down.

To inspect your exhaust system you will need:

■ **A jack, jackstands, and wheel chocks**—To raise the vehicle.

■ **Rust penetrant**—To free up rusty and corroded nuts and bolts on clamps and hangers.

■ **Socket and combination wrenches**—10-mm and 12-mm for metric cars, 1/2-inch and 9/16-inch for domestics—to tighten loose clamps and hangers.

Check the undersides of all exhaust components for holes, blisters, loose flakes, or whitish deposits that result from corrosion. Tap each pipe and muffler—but not the catalytic converter—with a wrench. Good parts will make a ringing sound. Poor parts will make a dull thud.

Check all pipe connections for gaps or looseness and dark feathery streaks that indicate exhaust leaks. Tighten all loose nuts and bolts after first spraying them with rust penetrant.

Check all heat shields to see that there is at least a 1/2 inch air space between a shield and any nearby components. Carefully straighten any bent shields to achieve correct clearance. Check for cracks in the shields and brackets. They can cause annoying rattles and vibrations.

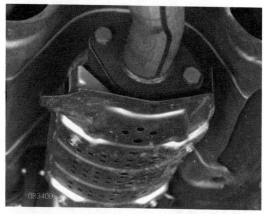

Check rubber hangers for damage and deterioration. Replace any bad ones immediately. Unsupported weight, such as that of the muffler, can cause a great deal of expensive damage to the system.

Spray all nuts and bolts with rust penetrant. It dissolves existing rust and slows the formation of new corrosion. This will make it easy to tighten nuts and bolts or to remove them when work is needed.

A NOTE ON MUFFLER AND TAILPIPE REPLACEMENT

Other than replacing muffler and tailpipe hangers, which is an easy job, exhaust system work can be difficult. Old exhaust systems don't like to come apart where they're supposed to. Flanged connections aren't much of a problem, although their nuts and bolts must occasionally be cut off. Slip joints, however, are often impossible to separate, particularly when they were assembled correctly with joint sealing compound.

When you weigh the labor cost of $35 to $50, depending on the complexity of your system, against the struggle you face if you do the work yourself, the savings is not terribly attractive. This is definitely a DIFM job—Do It For Me.

Section 12:

Body

HOW TO REPLACE WINDSHIELD WIPERS

We consider regular inspection and replacement of windshield wipers to be an essential part of body maintenance. Windshield wipers deteriorate whether they're being used or not. The rubber squeegees become brittle from exposure to sunlight and pollution.

To be certain your wipers are in good condition, test them every time you wash your vehicle. While the windshield is still wet, clean the edge of the squeegee, and operate the wipers. They should completely wipe the water off of the windshield, leaving no sheeting or streaks. If the wiper path is not completely clear, the blades should be replaced.

Hidden wipers are easier to work on when they are "parked" on the windshield. First wet the windshield, then turn the ignition switch to ON and turn on the wipers. When the wipers are halfway up, turn off the ignition switch and the wipers will stay up.

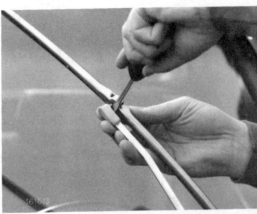

To replace an entire pin-mount wiper assembly, disconnect it from the arm by carefully twisting a screwdriver between the arm and the wiper. Install the new wiper by pushing it onto the pin until it locks in place.

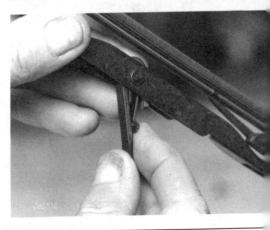

To replace an entire hook-mount wiper assembly, press in on the lock tab and slide the wiper out of the hook on the end of the arm. Slide the new wiper mount into the hook until it locks in place.

To replace just the wiper blade insert, compress the spring lock with pliers and slide the insert out of the arm.

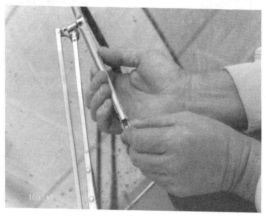

Slide the new insert into the blade, making sure it's connected to each of the little arm ends. Lock the insert in place by pushing it into the end of the arm until the locks open. Check to make sure the insert is engaged with all the arm ends.

Lube, Oil, & Chassis Service

HOW TO LUBRICATE HINGES AND LATCHES

Cars and trucks have a number of pivots, hinges, and latches that require lubrication to operate properly. A couple of times a year is usually enough. With 10 to 15 minutes of easy work you'll have all the latches working like new, and the hinges probably won't make a sound!

To do a first-rate job you will need:

- **White lithium grease**—For door and hood hinges and latch plates.

- **Stainless stick lubricant**—For door, trunk, and hatch strikers that you might brush against getting in and out of the car. This is a colorless lube that doesn't attract dirt like grease does.

- **Powdered graphite lubricant**—For door locks. This stuff won't gum up with dust or freeze in cold weather.

- **Vinyl protectant**—For weatherstripping. This will keep seals supple and allow them to work the way they should.

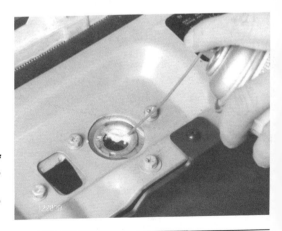

Spray a small amount of white lithium grease onto the hood latch plate, and between the plate and the latch body.

Apply stainless stick lubricant to the contact area of the hood latch striker and to the safety latch.

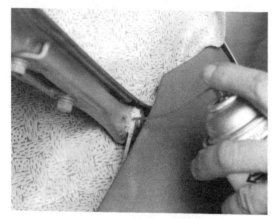

Spray white lithium grease into the hinge openings. Place a rag behind the hinge to catch overspray.

Hold the lock seals open with the key, and squeeze in a few puffs of graphite lubricant. Insert the key fully, and lock and unlock it several times to distribute the graphite.

Lube, Oil, & Chassis Service

Spray white lithium grease into the upper and lower hinge pins, and onto the top and underside of the door detent bars.

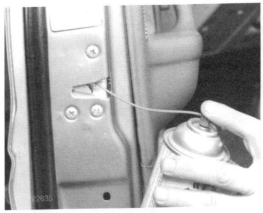

Spray white lithium grease into the latch mechanism of each door. Wipe any excess from the door edges.

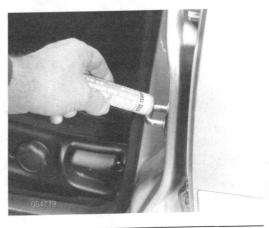

Apply stainless stick lubricant to the top and bottom of door and trunk strikers. Strikers can ruin a lot of clothes if they are lubed with anything other than stainless stick lube.

160

Lubricate and protect the rubber door seals with vinyl protectant. There are several brands that are specially compounded for weatherstripping and seals, and when properly used they can help make soft rubber and vinyl parts last for the life of the vehicle.

For truck and station wagon tailgates, spray white lithium grease into the latch mechanisms on each side of the tailgate. Then, wipe away any excess that might attract dirt.

Lubricate the strikers on each side of the tailgate opening with white lithium grease.

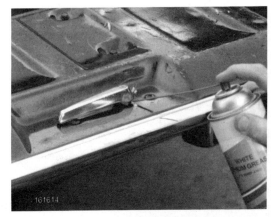

Spray white lithium grease *on the pivot points in the tailgate handle mechanism.*

Lubricate the tailgate hinges with white lithium grease. *Work the tailgate up and down several times to distribute the grease, and wipe off any excess.*

MAINTENANCE LOG

Date/Mileage	Work Performed	Parts/Supplies Used*	Cost

*Keep your receipts

Date/Mileage	Work Performed	Parts/Supplies Used*	Cost

*Keep your receipts

Date/Mileage	Work Performed	Parts/Supplies Used*	Cost

*Keep your receipts

Date/Mileage	Work Performed	Parts/Supplies Used*	Cost

*Keep your receipts

INDEX

A

Additives for oil 25-28

Alternator, see Drive belts

Antifreeze

    Amount needed 14

    Freeze protection versus concentration 120

    Procedure for mixing with water 118-119

API rating of oil 10

Asbestos brake dust, Pro Tip on dangers of 126

ATF, see Automatic transmission fluid

Automatic transmission fluid 13, 65

    Adding 67

    Change interval 70

    Checking level and condition 65-66

    Danger of overfilling 69

    Pro Tip on checking for contamination 68-69

Automatic transmission

    Damage caused by coolant leak 68-69

    Draining fluid 70

    Fluid and filter change procedure 70-74

    Pan bolt tightening 74

    Pan gasket 71, 73

    Pro Tip on how to remove fluid if accidentally overfilled 69

    Secret of leak-free service 73

B

Ball joints

    Inspection 51-52

    Lubrication 52

Bleeding brakes, see Brake system

Body hinges and latches, lubrication 158-162

Boots

    CV-joint, replacement procedure 56-59

    Inspection 50

Brake bleeder wrench 15

Brake cleaner 17

Brake dust, Pro Tip on dangers of 126

Brake fluid

    Bleeding or flushing, see Brake system

    Danger of contamination with water 121

    Inspecting and adding 121-123

    Interval for change 122

    Pro Tip on how fluid level indicates brake wear 124

    Specification 123

    Types 15

Brake system

    Bleeding procedure 130-134

    Flushing and replacing fluid 135

Brakes, disc, see Disc brakes

Bump stops, Pro Tip on checking 53

Bushings, Pro Tip on replacement 60-61

C

Control arms, inspection 51

Coolant

    Adding 104

    Checking level and condition
       103-104

Cooling system

    Antifreeze concentration required
       for freeze protection 120

    Coolant, see Coolant

    Flushing procedure 115-116

    How to remove the radiator cap
       102

    List of tasks in complete "tune-up"
       service 101-102

    Must be cold before opening 102

    Operating temperature 106

    Pressure testing 106-107

    Pro Tip on installing a flushing
       fitting 117

    Refilling procedure 118-119

    Thermostat, see Thermostat

Cooling system flush 13

Cooling system flushing kit 14

Crankcase, draining oil 41

CV-joint

    Boot replacement, see Boots

    Description 85-86

D

Dexron, see Automatic transmission
    fluid

Dipstick 31-32, 35, 47

Disc brakes

    Inspection procedure 125-127

    Pad thickness 126

    Pro Tip on why they squeal and
      how to fix 128-129

    Rotor inspection 127

    Wear indicator 128

Door lock lubrication 159

DOT Type 3, see Brake fluid

Drain pan 11

Drain plug, washer and installation 44

Drain plug washers, buying tips 10

Drive belts 13

    Checking condition and tension
      94

    Pro Tip on saving old belts for
      road-emergency kit 100

    Pro Tip on types, specs, and
      length 98-100

    Replacement procedure 95-97

    Tightening 95-96

Driveshaft U-joint inspection and
    lubrication 76-77

E

Emission control system, Pro Tip on
    warranty coverage 7-8

Exhaust system, inspection procedure
    151-154

Exhaust system, muffler and tailpipe
    replacement 154

T

Thermostat 15

    Operation 108

    Replacement procedure 108-111

Torsion bars, Pro Tip on checking 62

Transmission, see Manual
  transmission or Automatic
  transmission

W

Warranty

    Maintenance records required 5

    Pro Tip on emission control
      system warranty 7-8

Wheel bearings,

    Grease seals 12

    Service and lubrication procedure
      78-84

    Types of front bearings 78-79

    Types of rear bearings 79-80

Wheel-bearing grease, see
  High-temperature grease

Windshield wipers

    Blade inserts 17

    Replacement 155-157

COLOPHON

As well as being automotive enthusiasts, we are also quality book enthusiasts. The word colophon is from the Greek kolophon, meaning "summit, or finishing touch." We include one in this book because we know that many of you are interested in such things. Besides, this is a bit of tradition that we wish to perpetuate!

Type: The Helvetica family was chosen because of its excellent legibility and friendly appearance. The body type of this book is 10/12 Helvetica. Photo and illustration captions are 9/11 Helvetica-Bold and -Light. Captions are in Helvetica Black.

Photos: To eliminate harsh shadows, indoor shots were done with indirect umbrella lighting, and outdoor shots were done in open north-facing shade. Wherever possible, we show the reader's point of view and very close detail. Film developing and printing was done by The Darkroom, a professional lab in Northridge, California.

Illustrations: Illustrations were drawn from photo reference to ensure accuracy. We chose to include Mr. Amos' hand lettering because of its warmth and clarity.

Electronic page production: Manuscripts were prepared and edited in XyWrite on a 386 PC. Illustrations were scanned on a Microtek 300Z. Page layout, illustration sizing and cropping, and all typesetting was done on a 386 PC with Ventura 3.0 for Windows. Other important software used in the production of this book included Corel Draw 2.0, Adobe ATM 1.0, the Adobe Type Library, and of course, Windows 3.0. Page proofs were "pulled" on an NEC890 Postscript laser printer, and final camera-ready output was done on a Linotronic 300 by Flying Color Graphics in Canoga Park, California.

Printing and binding: Performed by Griffin Printing, a unique environmentally sensitive, employee-owned company in Glendale, California. Photos were prepared as 120-line halftone negatives and were hand-stripped. The body of the book was printed on 50-pound offset paper on a Timson full-web heat-set press. Covers were printed on a four-color Heidelberg press and were UV coated for resistance to soiling.

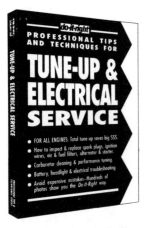

do-it-right

PROFESSIONAL TIPS AND TECHNIQUES FOR

TUNE-UP & ELECTRICAL SERVICE

- **FOR ALL ENGINES:** Total tune-up saves big $$$.
- How to inspect & replace spark plugs, ignition wires, air & fuel filters, alternator & starter.
- Carburetor cleaning & performance tuning.
- Battery, headlight & electrical troubleshooting.
- Avoid expensive mistakes—Hundreds of photos show you the *Do-It-Right* way.

This is a complete guide to two types of important DIY jobs.
Part A, Tune-Up, gives you a 5-step procedure for inspecting and tuning virtually any gasoline engine. Part B, Electrical Service, shows you how to perform a number of easy, money-saving electrical jobs.

192 pages, 219 illustrations
ISBN 1-879110-15-6

TUNE-UP CONTENTS: 1 Tune-Up Overview: • The correct steps and sequence for a tune-up • Tuning a modern electronic engine **2 Tune-Up Parts, Supplies and Tools:** • Examination of what you need **3 Valve Adjustment:** • How mechanical and hydraulic valve lifters work • How to fix noisy lifters **4 Compression Test:** • How to perform dry and wet compression tests • How to interpret test results **5 Spark Plugs:** • Reading engine condition • How to know if you need hotter or colder spark plugs • How to prepare and install new plugs **6 Distributor and Wires:** • How to test spark plug wires • How to assemble "universal" wire kits • How to install new ignition wires • How to inspect, test, and service the distributor • How to use a tach/dwell meter • How to check and adjust ignition timing **7 Carburetor/Fuel Injection:** • How to clean a carburetor • How to clean and inspect a fuel-injection system • How to replace the fuel filter(s) • How to inspect and test a PCV system • How to replace the air filter • How to adjust idle speed • Oldies only—fast-idle and mixture adjustment.

ELECTRICAL SERVICE CONTENTS:
8 Electrical Parts, Supplies and Tools: • A look at what you need **9 Battery:** • How a battery works and what can go wrong • How to inspect and service the battery • How to test condition with a hydrometer • How to select and replace • How to charge • How to measure and replace battery cables **10 Lamps and Wiring:** • How to replace sealed-beam and quartz-halogen headlamps • How to upgrade tungsten headlamps to quartz-halogen • How to aim headlamps • How to replace exterior and interior lamp bulbs • How to troubleshoot bulb burnout problems • How to replace damaged wires and sockets **11 Fuses and Circuit Breakers:** • How to inspect and replace fuses and fusible links • How to install an in-line fuse holder **12 Charging System:** • How to troubleshoot problems in the alternator and charging system • How to replace the alternator **13 Starting System:** • How to troubleshoot starter problems • How to replace the starter.

PROFESSIONAL TIPS AND TECHNIQUES FOR

DETAILING CARS & TRUCKS

- How to perform a $150 detail job in one day.
- How to restore dull paint, trim, tires & aluminum wheels—To better than new!
- Concours engine & interior detailing.
- 15-minute "speed wash" for less than a buck.
- Avoid expensive mistakes—Over 340 photos & illustrations show you the *Do-It-Right* way.

This is a book on complete appearance care—from routine washing and waxing to show-quality preparation.

192 pages, 388 illustrations
ISBN 1-879110-17-2

CONTENTS:

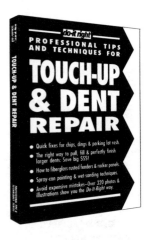

do-it-right
PROFESSIONAL TIPS
AND TECHNIQUES FOR

TOUCH-UP & DENT REPAIR

• Quick fixes for chips, dings & parking lot rash.
• The right way to pull, fill & perfectly finish larger dents: Save big $$$!
• How to fiberglass rusted fenders & rocker panels.
• Spray-can painting & wet-sanding techniques.
• Avoid expensive mistakes—Over 320 photos & illustrations show you the *Do-It-Right* way.

This book shows you how to do the easier types of body work and painting, from touch-up of minor chips and parking lot rash, to pulling and filling larger dents.

192 pages, 338 illustations
ISBN 1-879110-18-0

ORDER FORM & INFORMATION REQUEST

We recommend you purchase Do-It-Right books from your local retailer, where you purchased this book. But if you would like to order from us or add your name to our mailing list for future product announcements, please use this form.

Name: _____

Mail to:
Do-It-Right Publishing
Post Office Box 839
Newhall, CA 91322-0839

Address: _____

_____

Credit card orders, call toll-free:
1-800-223-3556
9-5 Pacific Time, Monday-Friday
(In California: **1-800-445-4944**)

City: _____ State: _____ Zip: _____

Daytime phone: _____
(in case we have to call about this order)

Title	Price Each	Quantity	Total
Tune-Up & Electrical Service	$8.95		
Lube, Oil & Chassis Service	$8.95		
Detailing Cars & Trucks	$8.95		
Touch-Up & Dent Repair	$8.95		
Total book order			
California residents: 6.5% tax (58¢ per book)			
Shipping & handling per order			$1.95
TOTAL AMOUNT			

Paid by: ❏ Check   ❏ Master Charge   ❏ Visa   ❏ American Express

Make checks payable to **Do-It-Right**.

Account No:_____ Expiration date: _____

Your Signature: _____

Orders are shipped immediately. Please allow several weeks for delivery.

❏ Please add me to your mailing list for new book and video announcements.

❏ Please send me a brochure on your model-specific factory-approved DIY manuals and shop manuals for: ❏ Nissan vehicles ❏ Hyundai vehicles.

Over for your comments.

Your comments on this *Lube, Oil & Chassis Service* manual would be appreciated.

_____

_____

_____

_____

I rate this book
❏ Excellent ❏ Very Good ❏ OK ❏ Poor

Other titles I would like to see from Do-It-Right:

_____ ❏ Book ❏ Video

_____ ❏ Book ❏ Video

FOLD HERE AND STAPLE OR TAPE SHUT

_____

_____

_____

```
PLACE
STAMP
HERE
```

Do-It-Right Publishing
Post Office Box 839
Newhall, CA 91322-0839

Do-It-Right Books are Different. Here is Why.

"After training factory technicians for 18 years, we wanted to bring the same type of concise job-specific training to DIYer's. This Professional Tips and Techniques Series is the result. We hope you enjoy it."

Photos and Illustrations Tell the Story. We believe that automotive instruction should be as *visual* as possible, because do-it-yourself work is a visual, hands-on process. We begin every book with a storyboard plan and a camera full of film. Our goal is to *show* you rather than to *tell* you how to do each job.

We Focus on Real-World Money-Saving Jobs. In our judgment, each job must (1) be easy for a DIYer to do with ordinary tools and skills, (2) have low risk of failure, and (3) be a meaningful money-saver. We assume that your prime motivation for DIY work is to save money!

Each Book is a Mini-Course. While certainly nothing like a school textbook, each book in this *Professional Tips and Techniques Series* provides an in-depth treatment of the jobs it covers. Each book builds your automotive knowledge and hands-on skills. Each book prepares you to attempt new tasks and produce quality results.

A "Good Read!" We are automotive enthusiasts, and we've tried to share that love with you! We've included a lot of background info on *why* jobs are done a certain way, rather than just giving you procedures to follow blindly. We've openly shared our opinions. And we've worked hard to bring you condensed, up-to-date, and interesting information for DIY work in the 90's.

If you would like to be notified of future Do-It-Right books and videos, please send us your name and address on the enclosed form. We welcome your suggestions and comments to help us improve our books.

Dennis Holmes
President
Do-It-Right Publishing

SHOPPING LIST

Oil Change
❏ Engine oil
   No. of quarts:
   w/filter ____ w/o filter ____
   Grade (SG or higher): ____
   Weight, SAE: 10W-30 ❏
   10W-40 ❏ 10W-50 ❏ 20W-50 ❏
   30W ❏ 40W ❏ 50W ❏
❏ Oil filter: No. ____
❏ Oil additive (if required)
❏ Drain plug washer
❏ Oil filter wrench

Chassis Lubrication
❏ Grease: ❏ Multipurpose
   ❏ High-temperature
❏ Manual transmission gear oil:
   Grade GL __
❏ Differential oil:
   Grade GL __
❏ Wheel bearing grease seals
❏ Automatic transmission funnel
❏ Grease gun
❏ CV joint grease fitting adapter

Automatic Transmission Service
❏ Automatic transmission fluid
   Type: DEXRON II ❏ F ❏
   No. of quarts: ____
❏ Transmission filter
❏ Transmission pan gasket
❏ Automatic transmission funnel

CV Boot Replacement
❏ CV boots (split type)
❏ CV joint grease

do-it-right

Cooling System Service
❏ Cooling system flush
❏ Antifreeze: No. of quarts ____
❏ Flushing fitting kit
❏ Radiator and heater hoses
❏ Hose clamps
❏ Thermostat
❏ Thermostat housing gasket
❏ RTV Sealer

Drive Belt Replacement
❏ Alternator belt
❏ Power steering belt
❏ Water pump belt
❏ A/C belt
❏ Other (specify) _____

Brake System Service
❏ Brake fluid
❏ Brake bleeder wrench
❏ Bleeder hose (clear plastic)

Shock Absorber Replacement
❏ Shock absorbers
❏ Rust penetrant

Body Service
❏ White lithium grease
❏ Graphite lubricant
❏ Stainless stick lubricant
❏ Windshield wiper blade inserts

General Tools & Supplies
❏ WD-40   ❏ Jack
❏ Brake cleaner ❏ Jackstands (2)
❏ Hand cleaner   ❏ Wheel chocks
❏ Funnels   ❏ Fender cover
❏ Drain pan   ❏ Goggles
❏ Shop rags